TOP 100 UNUSUAL THINGS TO SEE IN ONTARIO

Ontario's painted desert. Medina shale, dramatically exposed, in a 37-hectare hillside north of the village of Cheltenham.

TOP 100
UNUSUAL THINGS
TO SEE IN ONTARIO

RON BROWN

For Harold
Christmas 2005
from
Marna

The BOSTON MILLS PRESS

A BOSTON MILLS PRESS BOOK

First printing.

Library and Archives Canada Cataloguing in Publication

Brown, Ron, 1945-
Top 100 unusual things to see in Ontario / Ron Brown.

Includes index.
ISBN 1-55046-425-6

1. Ontario--Guidebooks. 2. Curiosities and wonders--Ontario--Guidebooks. I. Title.

FC3057 B78 2005 917.1304'5 C2005-902239-6

U.S. CIP data available upon request.

Published by Boston Mills Press
132 Main Street, Erin, Ontario, Canada N0B 1T0
Tel 519-833-2407 Fax 519-833-2195
e-mail: books@bostonmillspress.com
www.bostonmillspress.com

In Canada:
Distributed by Firefly Books Ltd.
66 Leek Crescent, Richmond Hill
Ontario, Canada L4B 1H1

In the United States:
Distributed by Firefly Books (U.S.) Inc.
P.O. Box 1338, Ellicott Station
Buffalo, New York, USA 14205

The publisher gratefully acknowledges the financial support for our publishing program by the Canada Council for the Arts, the Ontario Arts Council and the Government of Canada through the Book Publishing Industry Development Program.

Text and cover design by Chris McCorkindale and Sue Breen, McCorkindale Advertising & Design

Printed in China

CONTENTS

INTRODUCTION

Thomas Foster modelled his memorial to his wife after India's Taj Mahal.

Ontario is full of hidden treasure. Down village streets, in city lanes, and along quiet country roads lie its most unusual sights—houses that seem to float, a river that disappears, log cabins in the centre of a major city. All await the curious explorer. Monuments to murders, massacres and mysterious spy camps bring to life the lesser-known aspects of Ontario's hidden heritage.

This book features my pick of Ontario's top 100 unusual things to see. It combines the best features found in the *50 Unusual Things to See in Ontario* series, updates them and adds new oddities as well. Most of the listings are easy to see and are available to the public, either through admission, or from a public vantage point.

There is no particular order to the arrangement of the chapters in this volume, and that, in the opinion of this random explorer, is as it should be. Head out and discover whichever treasure appeals at the moment. Temples, towers and quirks of nature offer insight into an Ontario that few even know exists. And that's what looking for treasure is all about.

Ron Brown, Toronto

Ouimet Canyon, Ontario's miniature version of the Grand Canyon.

1

North America's longest single-span wooden bridge extends over the Sioux Narrows.

OVER THE SIOUX NARROWS:
North America's Longest Wooden Bridge

Sioux Narrows is an unlikely place to find the continent's biggest anything. A tiny tourist town of fewer than four hundred, Sioux Narrows straddles Highway 71 about 80 kilometres southeast of Kenora, Ontario. It also straddles the Sioux Narrows, an intriguingly named channel of water along the eastern shore of the Lake of the Woods. Although traditionally the territory of the Cree, the Lake of the Woods was subjected to frequent raids by the Sioux tribes, which lived to the south. Key defensive locations such as Sioux Narrows were often named to celebrate decisive victories over the intruders. According to legend, an entire flotilla of invading Sioux warriors was wiped out as they passed beneath the soaring cliffs by the narrows.

In the early years of the twentieth century, the gold mines and the lumber camps in the area attracted Europeans, who stayed and became settlers. With no railway nearby, the homesteaders relied on the lake steamers and a dirt trail to the south for transportation. In 1936, the Depression-era road-building program brought highway links to both the north and the south. Only the Sioux Narrows on the Lake of the Woods stood in the way of a through route.

Using creosoted Douglas fir from British Columbia, the highway engineers bridged the chasm, and in so doing gave Sioux Narrows its unusual claim to fame—the longest single-span wooden bridge in North America. Its main span, the Howe Truss, covers 64 metres, and the bridge's total length is more than 110 metres. It was situated high enough above the water to allow early steamships to pass beneath.

By 2003, the bridge had deteriorated to the point where large vehicles could no longer use it, and by 2004 it was closed to through traffic. It then became the subject of a petition that was organized to save the historic structure from replacement.

2

NICHOLSON:
A Ghost Town Worth Visiting

The province of Quebec can boast about its ghost-town park of Val Jalbert, while the state of Michigan can claim Fayette. But Ontario, with its many ghost towns, can make no such claim. Although it once came close.

Nicholson came from the vision of two determined entrepreneurs. Northerners James Austin and George Nicholson from Chapleau, a railway centre and the site of a sawmill, recognized the growing demand for timber for railway ties. On the shore of Windermere Lake, about 19 kilometres west of Chapleau, they built a mill to manufacture such ties. The bustling town, with two churches, a hotel, a store, a school and a boarding house, was for three decades home to 250 residents. When the mill burned in 1933, the town was largely abandoned.

Forty years later, a team of Ontario government historians visited the site. They parted the bushes and stared at the abandoned main street and overgrown cabins of the once-thriving town. The sight so impressed them that they recommended that Nicholson be preserved as a ghost-town park.

That might have happened except for two critical factors. First, the government department to which the historians reported was the Ontario Ministry of Natural Resources. Regarding the project as beyond its scope, the ministry ignored the recommendation. Then, shortly after the report was relegated to the shelves, a careless hunter accidentally set one of the flimsy structures ablaze. The ensuing inferno consumed most of what had been the main street, and with it, Ontario's hopes of having a ghost-town park.

Despite the destruction, the site remains one of the province's most striking ghost towns. Several of the old cabins can still be found, in use now as cottages. Others lie long abandoned, collapsing in the advancing forest. Visible, too, are the two-storey school and the former Catholic church, although both are now in a collapsed state.

Although it is possible to reach the site by VIA Rail's Sudbury-to-White River rail-liner, schedules no longer permit a same-day return. The simpler route to the site is by boat from Shoals Provincial Park, located on the south side of the lake.

If provincial decision-makers had acted years ago, Ontario, like Quebec and Michigan, could claim its own ghost-town park. Today, it's too late.

The ghost town of Nicholson almost became a ghost-town park.

3

DYER'S DEDICATION:
Muskoka's Wilderness Memorial

Calling Muskoka a "wilderness" anymore may be a stretch. With lakeside condos and country homes, it is now more a form of low-density sprawl enhanced by lakes and woodlands. But as you negotiate your car along the narrow road that leads to the Dyer Memorial, north of Huntsville, and the trees on either side close in, you might be forgiven for thinking that you are indeed in the wilds.

That's what it was when Clifton G. Dyer and his wife, Betsy, began visiting the area. They spent their honeymoon canoeing in Algonquin Park in 1916 and fell in love with the land. In 1940 they built a cottage on the Big East River, near Huntsville, returning every year to that wilderness retreat until 1956, when Betsy died.

Dyer was devoted to his wife, and in the year after her death he built a moving tribute to her. On the highest point on his property, overlooking their beloved river, he erected a 12-metre stone cairn. He surrounded it with a 390-square-metre flagstone terrace, and around that created a 4-hectare botanical garden. On the top of the cairn, in a copper urn, he placed his wife's ashes to rest. Following his own death, in 1959, his ashes were placed next to hers.

Although the public enjoys free access, Dyer's Memorial is on private property. The Dyer estate, which still maintains the cairn and garden, welcomes visitors, who in the summer may number two hundred a day. The memorial is located near the hamlet of Williamsport, about 10 kilometres northeast of Huntsville. Small arrows point the way.

Although Clifton Dyer's cottage was sold long ago, the wilderness memorial to his wife will survive with his dedication to her: "An affectionate, loyal and understanding wife is life's greatest gift."

Dyer's wilderness memorial.

CANADA'S GIBRALTAR:
Bon Echo Rock

Glowing gold and red in the rays of the evening sunset, and framed by pine and birch trees, Bon Echo Rock is a ready-made subject for a painting or a photograph. Rising from a geological fault line for 1.6 kilometres along Mazinaw Lake, this 91-metre cliff has acquired the nickname "Canada's Gibraltar."

Its appeal dates back a long time. For centuries, Native canoists paused at the foot of the sheer rock face and, using ochre and bear grease, painted their impression of the life they lived and the creatures they revered. These birds, mammals and even human figures are still portrayed in what is considered Ontario's largest-known collection of pictographs.

The place also appealed to Flora MacDonald Denison. In 1919, Denison, one of Ontario's earliest women's-rights advocates, bought the Bon Echo Inn. She transformed the resort into a retreat for Canadian artists and formed the Walt Whitman Club of Bon Echo. For many years the haven drew such artists as Group of Seven painter Franz Johnston, who sketched the cover of Denison's literary magazine, the *Sunset of Bon Echo*.

Following Whitman's death in 1919, Flora Denison added what has become the rock's most unusual feature—a tribute to the poet carved into the rock face. In letters a foot high are the words from his poem "Leaves of Grass."

> My foothold is tendon'd and mortised in granite
> I laugh at what you call dissolution,
> and I know amplitude of time.

The tribute is visible only from the water and is just north of the narrows that divide Upper and Lower Mazinaw Lake.

Bon Echo Provincial Park was created in 1959 after Flora Denison's son Merrill, English Canada's first important twentieth-century playwright, turned the site over to the Ontario government. It is eastern Ontario's largest provincial park and one of its most popular. Casual campers can drive to one of the more than five hundred campsites, while those seeking seclusion can canoe or hike to more remote locations. While rock climbers scale or rappell the sheer granite face, the more passive among us are content to simply stand at the narrows and paint, take photographs, or just try out the echo of Canada's Gibraltar.

The remarkable Bon Echo Park has been dubbed "Canada's Gibraltar."

5

GHOSTS OF THE GOLD FIELDS:
Ontario's Eldorado

The words "gold rush" conjure images of Barkerville, B.C., or the Klondike, with their boom-town buildings and barroom brawls. They scarcely evoke thoughts of southern Ontario, in particular the rugged hills north of Belleville.

Yet that is exactly where Ontario's first gold rush took place. It all began in 1866 when court clerk and part-time prospector Marcus Powell discovered a gold-laden cave on the farm of John Richardson. One nugget, he boasted, was the size of a butternut.

Once word got out, the rush was on. Grizzled gold seekers streamed in from as far away as the Cariboo Goldfields in British Columbia. And in the centre of the gold field, the boom town of Eldorado suddenly appeared. A shanty town of eighty buildings on muddy streets, it was as rough and tumble as any of its western counterparts. When sceptical prospectors, led by the notorious Cariboo Cameron, threatened to tear apart some of the mine buildings, twenty-five mounted police were quickly dispatched to keep order.

But they didn't need to stay long, for the gold rush was short-lived. Because the gold was chemically fixed to the parent rock, and impossible to mill using existing techniques, the only profit was through fraud. Disillusioned investors salted the claims with imported gold specimens and sold them to unsuspecting greenhorns.

Finally, about the turn of the century, a new milling process allowed extraction to begin and the overgrown mines sprang back to life. A few mills were erected, and the Central Ontario Railway added a simple wooden station. But even their second life was short, for the gold deposits were smaller than was first thought. After a few years of sputtering activity, the mines fell silent and Eldorado became a ghost town.

Hotels, former stores and even a few of the tiny miners' cabins dot the once-busy network of streets. Of the eighty or so original buildings, only two dozen survive, many with a decidedly boom-town air about them. The structures straddle a 1-kilometre section of Highway 62, a dozen kilometres north of Madoc. Here, a blue historic plaque commemorates Ontario's earliest golden boom town. But high up in the hills above the town, the roofless ruins of the early mills still lie, overgrown and uncelebrated.

Eldorado was the site of Ontario's first gold rush.

6

The disappearing Indian River.

THE DISAPPEARING RIVER OF PETERBOROUGH COUNTY

Now you see it, now you don't. After flowing wide and swift through the farmland of Peterborough County, the Indian River simply disappears. From its source in Dummer Lake, just south of Stoney Lake, the river meanders southward until, near the village of Warsaw, it enters an area of limestone and vanishes.

Limestone, as geologists will tell you, is noted for its solubility in water. Water not only erodes limestone, but can also dissolve it, creating spectacular caves and potholes in the rocks, known as kettles. But water is also able to seep between the porous layers of limestone and seemingly disappear, and that's just what the Indian River does.

Normally, rivers can flow through an area of limestone and stay in view. The Niagara River does. However, in the vicinity of Warsaw, a large outcrop of porous limestone blocks the flow of the river, and rather than go over or around the rock, the river has found enough cracks to simply flow through it.

From the parking lot in the Warsaw Caves Conservation Area, a path leads past kettles and caves to the river. As you cross the rock fall that blocks the river, you will notice something peculiar—the expanse of fast-flowing water swirls straight toward you and then disappears into the rock beneath your feet. You can hear the strange echoing gurgle of the water as the river makes its way underground. Beyond that point lies the now-dry former river bed, then about a half kilometre downstream the water bubbles back up to the surface to continue its course to Rice Lake.

A popular spot for picnickers, the park also offers a small beach, trails, and a network of caves for the cautious explorer. But it is the disappearing river that will provide you with the most vivid memory of this peculiar place.

THE RICE LAKE RAILWAY

In addition to its long-vanished stock of rice, Rice Lake is noted for its islands. Known popularly as "whalebacks," these rounded forms are the tops of underwater hills called drumlins. Sculpted into their smooth whaleback shapes by the glaciers that covered Ontario more than twenty thousand years ago, the oblong knolls line up to indicate the direction in which the great ice sheet flowed.

But among these whaleback islands is one that's strangely long and narrow, and it owes its origin not to the ice age, but to the railway age. In the early 1850s, Ontario's municipalities dropped all pretence at road building and put their money toward the latest transportation craze, the railway. Every town wanted one. Cobourg, on Lake Ontario, was no different. Its lake rival, Port Hope, was competing with Cobourg to obtain the first tracks to the interior. Rail lines that led inland could bring to the port lumber and farm products, especially barley, for export to the U.S. They could also bring much prosperity.

The link upon which Cobourg counted was chartered as the Cobourg and Peterborough Railway, with a link to the Chemong Lake Railway. But it faced one major construction obstacle: Rice Lake. For the railway to detour around the long, narrow lake would have been too costly, so it went straight across it. To do that, causeways were constructed from both shores and linked in the middle by a trestle, for a combined length of 5 kilometres. But the railway builders had not counted upon the force of the spring ice movements.

Year after year the ice damaged the trestle, and year after year the crews rebuilt it. Then, in 1860, while the Prince of Wales was visiting Ontario, his itinerary called for him to travel to Peterborough on the rail line. However, the trestle was considered too much of a risk for him to cross, and the following year the crossing was abandoned. Revenues were too paltry to justify its rebuilding.

The only freight worth carrying was iron from the mines further east, near Marmora, and even that was diverted onto barges that carried the ore from the lakeside village of Trent River to the railway's new Rice Lake terminus at Harwood.

By the turn of the century the mines had closed, and the link from Rice Lake to Cobourg was shut down soon after. Stations, rails and ties were all removed. The only evidence, besides the occasional bit of railbed, is the long thin "island" that stretches from Harwood into the water of Rice Lake, and the cribbings of the trestle that lurk perilously beneath the surface of the lake. The Harwood station was disassembled and rebuilt in the nearby town of Roseneath (with its historic carousel).

Use of the railway causeway over Rice Lake didn't last long.

8

Kingston's Martello towers provided a flexible but short-lived line of defence against the Americans.

KINGSTON'S LITTLE ROUND FORTS

For Ontario's history lovers, Kingston is as good as it gets. With its beautiful stone houses and institutional buildings (some dating from the 1790s), its historic forts, and the houses where Canada's first prime minister, Sir John A. Macdonald, slept, the city can keep a history buff occupied for weeks. But the structures that cause the most quizzical looks are the little round forts that seem to be almost everywhere.

Named Martello Towers after their role in repelling an attack at Cape Mortella on Corsica in 1796, these were the last word in defence. Their small size meant that they could be placed in defensive locations otherwise too small for a normal-sized fort. Their circular shape deflected cannon balls, and their high, small windows made them almost impossible to enter. They permitted a flexible line of defence and were almost impregnable.

Of the dozen or so built in Canada (Britain built about two hundred worldwide in the defence of the Empire) half are in Kingston. The oldest were the towers built in Halifax between 1796 and 1798; those in Kingston were added during the 1840s when the Oregon Crisis between Canada and the United States once again raised the spectre of American invasion. But the military usefulness of the forts in Kingston was relatively short-lived, as by 1860, newly introduced naval guns had the capacity to demolish the sturdy bastions with a single shot.

Of Canada's surviving Martello Towers, those in Kingston, with their distinctive roofs and their neat stonework, are considered the most appealing architecturally. All are readily visible. While two are connected to the museum fortress of Fort Henry, two others, the Murney Tower near Macdonald Park and Fort Frederick Tower, are both museums. The one at Fort Frederick was the only tower to be three storeys high, and is part of the Royal Military College. The third pair, those known as Shoal Tower and Cedar Island Tower, lie offshore.

DEATH BENEATH THE STREET:
Lemieux's Underground Death Trap

As the bus lurched along the winding road to St-Jean-Vianney, a suburb of Jonquière in central Quebec, its wipers smacked vainly at the sheets of rain that lashed the windshield. Suddenly something seemed terribly wrong. Ahead, where the road should have been there lay only darkness. The brakes couldn't hold on the slippery black pavement, and the bus slid helplessly into the gaping crater. Beside the road the ground buckled and heaved and then gave way, sucking thirty-six houses and their helpless inhabitants into it.

When the grey dawn finally broke, rescue workers could only gaze in amazement. Where the town once stood, there was now a gaping hole in the ground a quarter of a kilometre across and, at the bottom, a quagmire of watery clay with thirty-one victims buried in its depths.

These innocent men, women and children had fallen victim to a freakish subterranean phenomenon known as leda clay. A fine sediment, this clay, when dry, remains deceptively hard and firm. But when it becomes saturated after prolonged rain, it destabilizes and turns the consistency of quicksand.

The dramatic shots on TV and in the newspapers sent soil scientists and planners scuttling to identify areas where the deadly dirt might lurk. One such area lay along the banks of the South Nation River, southeast of Ottawa. Perched on top was the little village of Lemieux, a Franco-Ontarian farm village characterized by the silvery steeple of the Catholic church, its future seeming as stable as its past. Then on May 16, 1971, 16 hectares of a nearby pasture collapsed, so soil scientists decided to act. (Sensing the imminent danger, the cows had stubbornly refused enter the pasture, as was their daily custom.)

No one could say when the village would be next. So after warning the villagers of the deadly danger, the government began purchasing the village buildings. The last to go was the church, removed in 1992. Then, a little over a year later, mere metres from the old village yards, more than 3 million cubic metres of earth slipped into the river, carrying with it pasture, forest, a length of roadway and a pickup truck (the driver emerged safely).

Today, the road still ends a short distance from the village site. In the village itself are now only foundations, and a lonely stretch of sidewalk beside which the former villagers have placed a small cairn to commemorate their escape from the deadly dirt. The site is located 13 kilometres northeast of the town of Casselman.

The road to Lemieux slipped away and, along with farm fields, disappeared into the South Nation River.

10

IT CAME FROM OUTER SPACE:
The Holleford Meteor Crater

Most of us have at one time or another gazed in amazement at the night sky and watched streaks of light. On rare occasions we can hear the crackle as a "close one" burns up in the atmosphere. These are true visitors from outer space—meteors.

About twice a day, somewhere in Canada, a meteor thuds to the earth. Most are only about 100 grams in weight and make little impact; but a few have struck with a tremendous explosion, ripping apart the ground and leaving telltale circular craters or altered minerals.

To date, scientists have recorded about two dozen meteor craters in Canada. The 95-kilometre-wide strike in Sudbury is Canada's largest. The impact of what must have been an enormous meteor was so broad and deep that it completely altered the mineralization of the bedrock and created Canada's greatest nickel deposit.

Of the five meteor craters in Ontario (others are near Brent in Algonquin Park, at Wanapitei Lake west of Sudbury, and at the Slate Islands in Lake Superior) that at Holleford, north of Kingston, is the most readily visible from the ground. It was first discovered in 1955 by a team of scientists at the Dominion Observatory in Ottawa by poring over aerial photographs. Later research concluded that the extraterrestrial interloper must have arrived around 550 million years ago and measured 90 metres across. Exploding into the ground at an estimated 55,000 kilometres an hour, it has left a crater 2.35 kilometres in diameter and 30 metres deep.

To reach it, drive to Hartington on Highway 38, about 25 kilometres north of Exit 611 on Highway 401. From the centre of the village take the Holleford Road east for about 3 kilometres and follow the road as it bends to the north (left). Another 1.5 kilometres brings you to a T intersection, where you turn right. Then, after another 1.6 kilometres, the road descends a slope. This is the southwest wall of the crater. The road continues east along the slope of the crater for another kilometre to the Crater Farm and the one-time hamlet of Holleford, where a plaque stands by the fence on the north side of the road.

As with most meteor craters in Canada, erosion has softened its features and vegetation covers much of its slope. Yet it is hard not to stand and wonder at how the ground must have shaken when this visitor from outer space thundered to Earth.

This crater in the ground occurred when a meteor exploded into the Earth's crust.

11

SMITHS FALLS' HIGH-RISE PRIVY

Few of today's generation know much of that grand Canadian institution, the outhouse. Yet, for many generations of Canadians, that early-morning trek to the frigid wooden seat was as much a part of everyday life as a warm morning shower is today.

Privies are rare nowadays. But even when they were standard equipment, a two-storey outhouse was almost unheard of, unless you lived in Smiths Falls, Ontario.

In the 1850s, Joshua Bates, a Smiths Falls miller, chose a site next to his Rideau River grist mill to build a house. No ordinary house, it had some unusual features—an indoor brick bake oven, mirror-image facades and an outhouse that was two storeys high.

The logistics of how a two-storey outhouse might function without unpleasant consequences for the lower occupant are not readily apparent. A closer look, however, solves the riddle. Unlike most, this privy is connected to the house itself. The structure is wide enough that the upper facility need not be located directly above the lower one. In fact, a vertical partition separates the upper facility on one side from the lower facility on the other. While the door to the lower chamber leads directly off the downstairs porch, that to the upper room leads from an upstairs hallway. Simple, when you think about it.

In 1977 the town purchased the outhouse and the house attached to it and created a museum, restoring it to an 1867 appearance. Now known as the Heritage House Museum, it is located at 11 Old Sly's Road, in the southeast part of Smiths Falls.

While you're in town, be sure to visit the beautifully restored Canadian Northern Railway station at 90 Victoria Street, now a railway museum. More recently, the former Canadian Pacific Railway (CPR) station at 62 Victoria Street has been converted to a community theatre, while retaining a waiting room for VIA Rail train passengers.

At first glance this two-storey outhouse in Smiths Falls defies logic.

TRENTON'S BIG BOULDER

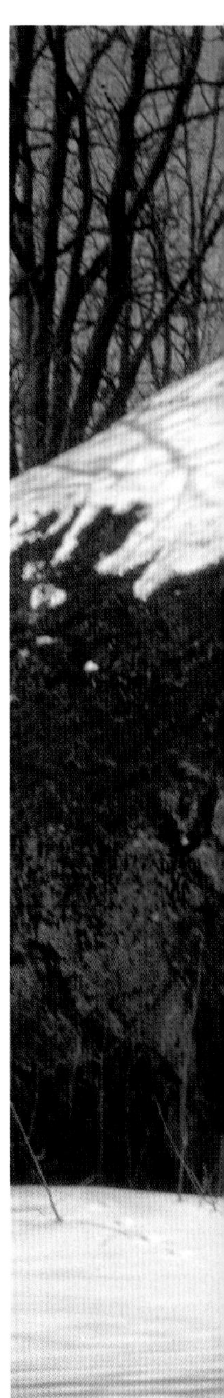

While clawing boulder after boulder from their fields, many early farmers curse the last ice age, claiming bitterly that all they harvest each year is a new crop of rocks. And they aren't far wrong. For in fields infested with boulders, the freezing and thawing of the ground in the spring in fact squeezes a fresh crop of boulders from beneath the surface.

Most such rocks were deposited during the last ice age, which some scientists claim covered Ontario to a depth of more than a kilometre. As the ice sheets cracked and began to melt about twenty thousand years ago, the torrents of meltwater spewed sand, gravel and rocks into the gaping crevasses. In central Ontario, the ice sheet melted in a long line where the glacial debris formed a ridge of rocky and sandy hills, a bouldery line that stretches from Orangeville in the west to Trenton in east. The deposit is widely known today as the Oak Ridges Moraine.

But it was at Trenton that the ice disgorged its biggest boulder, one the size of a house. Geologists call it the Glen Miller Erratic, their name for boulders that the ice sheets carried far from their parent bedrock. In Glen Miller, the Trenton suburb where it sits, residents simply call the Bleasdell Boulder.

Its veins of quartz and granite suggest that it has travelled a long distance from its origin in the Canadian Shield far to the north, a testament to the power of the great glaciers. And despite the young forest now surrounding it, the huge stone towers well above the humbled viewer. In fact it contains its own cave, large enough for a person to stand upright. The big boulder sits along a privately maintained trail located behind the Big Rock Café on Highway 33, north of Trenton.

Trenton's Big Boulder testifies to the awesome power of the glaciers that covered Ontario during the last ice age.

Trains once rambled under the town of Brockville to reach this tunnel.

RAILS UNDER BROCKVILLE:
Canada's Oldest Railway Tunnel

They said, "Every railway has to have a tunnel," so the builders of Ontario's earliest railway, the Brockville and Ottawa (B and O), built one.

Until the 1850s, the colonies that would become Canada had relied on muddy pioneer roads and perilous water routes to move people and products. Railways had been operating for two decades in the U.S. and Britain, and in the mid-1850s Canadians decided that it was their turn. Although the Grand Trunk and the Great Western Railway both began operating in Ontario in the 1850s, neither at that time had a tunnel. The B and O Railway was designed to link the St. Lawrence River route with Ottawa and to tap the forests and farms between. And because the town of Brockville was built on a ledge of limestone that cut off the waterfront, the railway engineers decided to blast a tunnel.

Begun in 1854, the tunnel would stretch nearly a kilometre through the limestone mesa. On December 31, 1860, the first wood-burning steam locomotive puffed its way through the darkness, the dim glow from its kerosene headlamp barely illuminating the way. It was Canada's first railway tunnel and the envy of a soon-to-be nation on the verge of the railway era.

But the engineering miracle that was the old Brockville tunnel was later forgotten when, in 1889, the Grand Trunk began digging its 1,800-metre tunnel beneath the St. Clair River to link Sarnia, Ontario, with Port Huron, Michigan. It marked the first time that tunnel builders used compressed air, and the event was featured in newspapers and engineering journals around the world.

Meanwhile, back in Brockville, the engines of the B and O, and later those of the CPR, continued to rumble through the darkness of the old tunnel until use of the passage was discontinued in 1954. A separate spur continued to access the waterfront until 1970.

For many years, Brockville's braver youth would explore the dampened darkness, until the entrance was finally sealed. Today, the tunnel is a historic site controlled by the Brockville museum. Visitors can now venture once more into the tunnel during operating hours and see a nearby CPR caboose.

THE SWAMP THAT FEEDS THE WORLD:
The Amazing Holland Marsh

Like much that is unusual and interesting in Ontario, the Holland Marsh is paid scant attention by travellers. To most, the marsh is little more than the flat, black fields that flash past along Highway 400. Yet, for the driver who exits at Canal Road, the marsh becomes one of the most interesting bits of landscape, not just in Ontario, but in Canada.

It is the country's largest vegetable garden.

That wasn't the case around the turn of the century, when this post-glacial lake bed, with decayed plants 30 metres deep, was good for little else than growing marsh grasses to stuff into mattresses. Then, in 1904, a Bradford grocer named Watson convinced professor W. H. Day of the Ontario Agricultural College in Guelph to investigate the possibility of draining the swamp for vegetable production. All his studies and experiments pointed to the same thing—the swamp could become one of Canada's premier market-garden areas.

In 1925, the Ontario Department of Agriculture began to drain the bog. Canals and dikes enclosed both sides of the wide valley like huge brackets, diverting the water to Lake Simcoe, into which the river flows.

By 1930, the rich black soil was drained and ready for farming. The first farmers to arrive were eighteen Dutch families from Hamilton, Ontario, in 1934. Many others, including Russians and Poles, followed, and within a few years the one-time swamp had become one of North America's leading vegetable-producing areas. (The name "Holland" does not come from the Dutch settlers, but rather from Major A. Holland, the British surveyor who laid out the land in 1830.)

Canal Road, which skirts the northern rim of the marsh, provides the best look at the 2,900-hectare marsh. From Highway 9 to Yonge Street in Bradford, Canal Road follows the northerly of the two canals through a world of overhanging willows and still canal waters. It passes sprawling modern backsplits that contrast with the cabins and trailers that house the seasonal workers who pick the lettuce, potatoes, celery, parsnips, cabbage, cauliflower and the 120,000 tonnes of carrots that sprout each year from the fertile earth.

A view across the Holland Marsh as harvest season approaches.

THE COMFORT GIANT:
Canada's Biggest Maple Tree

One specimen of the tree that symbolizes Canada may be older than the nation itself. The Comfort Maple squats wide and solid beside a field near Welland, Ontario. It had been there for three hundred years when, in 1816, the Comfort family first settled the land. And there it has remained, its survival defying all the odds.

Ontario once boasted a magnificent forest cover. Oak, hemlock, beech and maple provided a cooling leafy canopy that assured a high water table, which in turn allowed the many rivers and streams to flow year-round—cascading streams that powered the countless pioneer mills. But that forest quickly vanished, for what fire and old age didn't claim, pioneer wood hewers did.

With the forest gone, the water table lowered and the streams dried up, turning the once-vibrant mill towns into ghost towns. But the Comfort Maple survived. With its girth of 8 metres and crown width of 28 metres, the 30-metre-high giant became a local attraction, and owner Earl Hampton Comfort set aside a piece of land solely for the preservation of his tree. In 1961, his sister Edna donated the tree and 4 hectares of land around it to the Niagara Region Conservation Authority.

Today the authority maintains about a half hectare of land, a parking lot, and a few benches. As the ancient tree ages, it has become necessary to support some of the branches with guy wires. The tree sits on Metler Road, west of Victoria Avenue, which leads south from Exit 57 on the Queen Elizabeth Way.

The Comfort Maple is said to be Canada's largest maple tree.

16

THE TOWNSEND EXPERIMENT

There is something peculiar about Townsend.

Along Highway 3, about 50 kilometres southwest of Hamilton, faded signs advertise lots for sale in a place called Townsend. After you drive a short distance down that side road, passing fields and barns as you travel, you suddenly find yourself on a four-lane boulevard. Branching off to the side are streets that twist and curve, lined with modern homes. Further on, you find a substantial seniors' residence and a town centre overlooking a pond. And then Townsend ends as abruptly as it began.

But look more closely. You will find that those suburban streets end in overgrown fields, that the avenues are strangely free of traffic, and that the town centre contains little more than drab offices. Welcome to Townsend, once touted as Ontario's grand community of the future.

In the 1970s, government planners decided that the sprawl engulfing the Toronto–Hamilton–Oshawa area was out of control and should be redirected to a series of regional growth centres. The decentralization, theorized the planners, would also help spread the prosperity of those years to less populated and less prosperous regions.

The planners chose an area of flat farmland near the shores of Lake Erie to build a modern and planned new town. By 1976 coloured maps showed a proposed community of one hundred thousand, with areas for recreation, housing and industry, while tree-lined trails would welcome hikers, cyclists, horseback riders, and cross-country skiers. There would be high schools, hospitals and supermarkets, all connected by public transit.

But at the centre of it all would be the community showcase—the town centre. Built to overlook a landscaped lake, the centre would contain four department stores, specialty shops, restaurants, churches, cinemas, an art gallery and a hotel. An apartment complex would house six thousand residents, and sports lovers from throughout the region would travel to a stadium and sports fields. The first phase would start in 1978 and accommodate five thousand people.

But somehow the dream city turned into a nightmare. When the Canadian economy plunged into a recession and inflation skyrocketed, industry stayed away. So did most of the hundred thousand future residents. In fact, Townsend never expanded beyond that first phase. The recreation trails are overgrown, no buses rumble along the streets, and the town centre contains only a few social service offices. The grandly named Town Centre Road ends abruptly in an overgrown farm field.

While Townsend is no ghost town, and looks much like any other well-maintained suburb, the sudden dead-ends, the silence, and the town's odd location in the midst of fields and barns are all evidence that the "dream city" never came true.

The partially finished new town of Townsend.

17

St. Catharines' forgotten railway tunnel
is part of its seaway legacy.

ST. CATHARINES' FORGOTTEN TUNNEL

St. Catharines, Ontario, is a place for ship watchers. Part of today's St. Lawrence Seaway system, the Welland Canal cuts through the city's eastern suburbs. And although many of the lift bridges still provide frustrating waits for drivers while the ships inch past, the canal is a delight for boat buffs. The best viewing areas include the Lock 3 viewing platform and interpretative centre, the Twin Locks viewing centre, and a park beside Lock 8 in Port Colborne.

St. Catharines is also a bonanza for history enthusiasts, for it is home, not just to the current Welland Canal, but to three predecessor canals as well. Throughout the city, trails and bicycle paths lead past the old stone locks and canals, reminders of an era when the largest schooners could fit crossways on a modern vessel and were pulled through the canal by horses.

The first Welland Canal was opened in 1829, and the third canal was replaced in 1930 by much of the fourth, or current, canal. In the 1970s, yet another channel was blasted into the ground to bypass downtown Welland.

While many of the old canal structures are well indicated in heritage hiking brochures, one of the hidden treasures of the old canal age is the long-abandoned Grand Trunk Railway tunnel, which carried the trains beneath the third Welland Canal.

Built between 1875 and 1881, the tunnel was used for less than twenty years and was replaced by a bridge over the canal. Today it lies forgotten and uncelebrated, except by a few die-hard history enthusiasts, behind a tangle of trees. In the darkness, only a trickle of water passes where steam locomotives once puffed. The graceful limestone arch that marks the entrance remains as a lasting monument to the workmanship of the railway builders of the nineteenth century.

You can drive to the path that leads to the tunnel by following the Seaway Haulage Road south for 2 kilometres from Glendale Road in the eastern end of St. Catharines. From the guardrail on the western side of the road, a path leads into the ravine and the forgotten tunnel. In the pond on the eastern side of the road, you will also find some of the long-abandoned lock structures of the third canal itself.

DWARF CEDARS:
Ontario's Oldest Trees

Think of an old-growth forest and you think of redwood trees that soar upward until their tops disappear in a canopy of green. You don't envisage gnarly little cedars that twist out of the side of a rock and extend only 3 or 4 metres into the air. Yet these spindly little survivors are Ontario's oldest trees.

Normally a swamp species, the eastern white cedars are found along the lip of the Niagara Escarpment, some of them dating back more than six hundred years, and one nearly a thousand years. Dating such a tree is not an easy job. It requires boring into the trunk and then counting, often with the aid of a microscope, the hundreds of nearly invisible rings concentrated into the span of a hand.

Starting as seeds lodged in the limestone crevices centuries ago, the saplings edged slowly outward and then bent upward to face the warm and nutritious sunlight. Anchored in the stony depths, with no soil to feed them, the trees grew imperceptibly. But at least they grew. Their inaccessible location on the side of the cliff spared them from loggers, farmers and browsing animals, and even from the encroachment of other tree species. While original forests were falling all across Canada, the sturdy little white cedars sat firm and continued their slow growth skyward.

Thanks to the creation of a series of provincial parks, and a UNESCO designation as a World Biosphere Reserve, much of the Niagara Escarpment is finally available to the public. One of the best sites from which to view the ancient trees is in the conservation area at Rattlesnake Point. A short path leads from the parking area to the trail along the brink, where a stone fence protects careless walkers from a dangerous and likely deadly tumble over the precipice. It also allows an easy view of the old trees.

They can be identified by their light green, flat cedar needles, and by their trademark origin in the side of the cliff face. But as for the age of those that you see, only a bore sample and tedious tally of the tiny rings can tell you if the tree is sixty or six hundred years old.

Ontario's oldest trees are also among its smallest.

ONTARIO'S TAJ MAHAL:
The Thomas Foster Memorial

You don't need to spend a lot of time looking for this one; it dominates the countryside on County Road 1 about 2 kilometres north of Uxbridge. Thomas Foster was born near Toronto in 1852 and moved to the hamlet of Leaskdale, north of Uxbridge, where he ran the local hotel. He later moved back to Toronto, where he was elected a member of Parliament and later mayor of the city. One of his oddest acts was to offer a prize to the woman who could bear the most children in a ten-year period. But it was in real estate that he became one of its wealthiest citizens.

Following the death of his wife, he travelled the world. While visiting India he gazed in wonder at the beautiful Taj Mahal, built in 1628 by Shah Jahan as a monument to his wife, Mumtaz Mahal. Foster decided that he, too, would build a Taj-like temple for his own wife. The location he chose was a hilltop just north of Uxbridge and not far from his home town of Leaskdale.

In 1934 he commissioned architects J. H. Craig and H. H. Madill to design the memorial. Workers cleared away the hilltop and then began carefully laying limestone and marble according to the intricate plan. When they were done, the strange Byzantine monument rose more than 18 metres into the air. The onion dome was built of copper and allowed the sun to filter through twelve stained-glass windows. The coloured rays fell upon marble mosaics, lighting up the pink, green and black inlays on the walls and floor. Surrounding the floor are marble pillars, each different from the other. Against one wall stand the three crypts: his, that of his wife, and the third containing his daughter.

Maintained by the Foster Memorial Committee, and designated as a heritage building, the memorial plays host to weddings and plays, and is open to the public on the first and third Sunday of each month through the summer.

Thomas Foster modelled his memorial to his wife after India's Taj Mahal.

BELFOUNTAIN PARK:
The Stamp Man's Legacy

Under the gaze of a small cannon, the west branch of the Credit River plunges over a 10-metre waterfall and then tumbles down a rocky canyon. Beside the cannon are winding pathways lined with elaborate stonework, a chapel-like cave with the name Yellowstone, and a stone fountain with a bell on top.

This is the Belfountain Conservation Area. The creation of millionaire philanthropist, Charles W. Mack, it is one of Ontario's most unusual parks. Better known as the industrialist who invented and then manufactured the cushion stamp, Mack purchased this property on the rocky bank of the Credit River in 1908. Here, by the site of an early grist mill and quarry, he built a summer home for himself and his wife, and they named it Luck-e-nuf. He then hired master landscaper Sam Brock to create a park.

When finished, Brock had created a wonderland in stone. His park contained a dam for swimming, a lookout point, and a cave that he had converted into a chapel-like room. He had slung a suspension bridge across the canyon and topped it all off with a stone fountain with a bell on top, to commemorate the name of the village.

Belfountain, which lines the canyon rim, began in 1825 as a pioneer settlement named McCurdy's Village. During the 1860s it became home to mining company executives who managed the stone quarries in the Credit Canyon below. By the time Mack showed up, the mines had closed, and the miners' villages of Brimstone and Forks of the Credit had become ghost towns.

But Mack's park was quite popular, for when he had finished it, he opened the grounds to the public. Visitors could come to picnic, hike or swim, provided that they obeyed Charles Mack's rules: no swimming on Sundays, and men were to wear swim tops and women skirts at all times.

After Mack's death in 1943, his park was sold and was operated as a commercial business until 1955, when the Credit Valley Conservation Authority purchased the property. Additional acquisitions between 1961 and 1973 have given the grounds more space for picnicking, longer hiking trails and indoor washrooms.

Although Mack's modest cottage and cabin have been reduced to their foundations, most of Brock's handiwork remains in place. You can look into the Yellowstone cave, watch the waterfall from the lookout, cross the canyon on a newer bridge, or simply sit by the fountain with the bell on top.

Beautiful Belfountain Park was once a private estate.

21

GUIDING LIGHT:
Beautiful Point Abino Lighthouse

Perhaps it is because most of them lie on isolated shorelines, out of view of most landlubbers, that lighthouses are among the least appreciated of Ontario's heritage structures.

Some are small and squat, made of wood; others are tall and elegant, constructed of stone or brick. Then there is the lighthouse at Point Abino. Built of poured concrete, it is unlike any other lighthouse in Ontario. Constructed in a form of architecture known as Greek Revival, it is easily the most elegant lighthouse along the Ontario side of the Great Lakes.

Point Abino is located on Lake Erie just west of Fort Erie. With the urban boom that engulfed southern Ontario and upper New York State in the late 1800s, increasing numbers of city dwellers sought out the beaches and breezes of the nearest lakeshores. These numbers swelled following the opening of the Peace Bridge between Buffalo and Fort Erie in 1927. While more modest cottages and cabins crowded the beaches in nearby Crystal Beach, the forested peninsula at Point Abino became the exclusive enclave of wealthy industrialists. Families from New York and Ohio like the Rich family, owners of Rich products, and the Baird family, owners of the *Buffalo News*, erected grand summer homes here.

The lighthouse was completed in 1918, built to replace a light ship that was destroyed in a storm in 1913, killing all on board. A light-keeper's residence was added in 1921. Prior to the light ship, the dangerous shelf of rock, which creeps out from the point into the lake, was marked only by buoys. Because the light was surrounded by water and private homes, the keepers had to access the dwelling by wading through the shallows.

Ontario has a rich lighthouse legacy. During the late 1800s the government built around the shores of Lake Huron half a dozen lofty stone structures that they termed the "Imperial Towers." Of the six, that at Cape Rich, near Southampton, is the most accessible. The squat stone lighthouse from the Duck Islands has been moved to the Mariners Museum near Picton, Ontario. Port Rowan lays claim to having Ontario's oldest wooden lighthouse, and other lighthouses can be visited in Kincardine, on Long Point in Prince Edward County, on the Toronto Islands, and at Wingfield Basin, near Tobermory. The province of Quebec also promotes a "lighthouse route" along the shores of the lower St. Lawrence River.

Although no lighthouse in Ontario remains permanently staffed, most are still in use; the light at Point Abino light was last to be automated. The light has been declared a National Historic Site, and in 2001 was purchased by the town of Fort Erie. Sadly, that doesn't mean that you can visit it. Those same wealthy, mostly American families who own the surrounding property also own the road and have gated the entrance and staffed it with a security guard. Canadians thus cannot see one of their own historic sites, although tours are occasionally organized during the summer months.

The Point Abino lighthouse is easily the most elegant on the Ontario shores of the Great Lakes.

ROCKWOOD'S POTHOLES

Most communities don't like to brag about their potholes, especially when they're 6 metres wide and 12 metres deep and number almost two hundred. Rockwood, Ontario, about 12 kilometres northeast of Guelph, is different. Residents not only boast of their potholes, but have created a park for them!

The reason for this pride is that the potholes are not a result of neglected roads, but are a fascinating creation of nature. Sedimentary rocks such as limestone or sandstone are among nature's softest. Easily eroded, they can be sculpted and washed by wind and water into a fairyland of shapes. Caves, natural bridges and rock pillars are but a few of the shapes that the rock can assume.

Potholes are another form, occurring when boulders become trapped in the swirling eddies of fast-flowing rivers. As the boulders swirl around, they etch a hole in the bedrock beneath. Thousands of years must pass for the rocks to grind a hole even the size of a stew pot. Tens of thousands of years were required to form those at Rockwood.

This natural wonder is preserved in the Rockwood Conservation Area, on the western outskirts of the town. Trails lead from the parking lot up cliffs, past caves and even beside the ruins of a massive stone woollen mill and finally to the potholes themselves. Here, the Eramosa River flows though a watery labyrinth of potholes, some of which have collapsed, while others have eroded through. Other potholes remain high and dry and lurk darkly beneath the forest vegetation.

The most interesting way to explore them is to rent a canoe and coast lazily through the watery maze. You'll see potholes as you've never seen them before.

Rockwood's potholes.

Lemonville's mansions are set in a watery wonderland.

THE FLOATING MANSIONS OF LEMONVILLE

It's a watery wonderland, but one that's a long way from any river or lake. Lemonville sits on the slope of a sandy hill, the grey apartment towers and suburban glass offices of northeastern Toronto looming on the hazy horizon. An undistinguished hamlet that dates from pioneer days, Lemonville has in the past twenty years seen a most unusual housing boom—mansions that float on water, or so they appear.

The water comes not from a river or a lake, but from a massive and mysterious underground reservoir. The ridge that looms behind the mansions is known as the Oak Ridge Moraine. A line of sandy hills, it was formed when the great glaciers that once covered Ontario cracked and began to melt. The icy meltwater carried sand and rocks into a long fissure in the ice, and by the time the glacier had melted, all that remained was the long ridge.

Because the soil in the hills is so porous, rainwater drains right through it, creating a high water table at the foot of the hills. That is not unusual, but the Lemonville area sits on a geological anomaly. While the water seeps quickly through the light, sandy upper soils of the ridge, the flow suddenly encounters a hard subsurface layer of clay. This propels it even faster towards the flats below and keeps the water near the surface like a massive underground lake contained only by the soil above it. Because of the downward force of the water in the hills behind, whenever the surface of the flats is broken, the water gushes upward like a geyser unleashed.

But house builders have turned what could have been a curse into a blessing. By digging carefully into the underground lake, they have landscaped the large housing lots into a miniature lake land. Surrounded by ponds, some more than a hectare in area, are mansions in styles that range from "California ranch" to "Woodbridge Italianate," or simply to "Scarborough suburban." So popular are the little lakes that house prices often exceed $1 million.

The land of the floating mansion extends south on McCowan Road for about a kilometre from Bethesda Road and 2 kilometres west along Bethesda Road to Kennedy Road. Beside McCowan Road, one particularly large pond boasts a sign announcing "Downtown Lemonville."

AN INDUSTRIAL SURVIVOR:
Toronto's Gooderham and Worts Distillery District

Despite a history of insensitive and often unnecessary demolitions, Toronto can still claim a remarkable collection of heritage buildings. While structures like Old City Hall, Casa Loma and Union Station are widely known grand buildings, gritty industrial survivors are just as compelling and sometimes even more so.

Of paramount importance to Toronto's industrial heritage is the Gooderham and Worts complex at Parliament and Mill streets, in what was once the industrial heartland of east-end Toronto. Today it has been rechristened as "the Distillery District," and is Toronto's newest major tourist attraction. It is also considered Canada's oldest and most complete early-nineteenth-century industrial complex.

In the 1830s, English miller James Worts chose the confluence of the Don River with Toronto's harbour to erect a wind-powered flour mill, eastern Toronto's first industry. He was later joined by his brother-in-law, William Gooderham. It was common in pioneer Canada to use second-grade grain from grist-mill operations to produce whisky. And the Gooderham and Worts mill did just that.

In the 1850s both the Great Western Railway and Grand Trunk Railway completed their lines into Toronto, and the waterfront boomed with industry. In 1859, Gooderham and Worts added a magnificent limestone distillery, the beginning of an expansion phase that lasted until 1890. By 1861 the company was producing 6,000 gallons of whisky a day, and by 1870 it was responsible for one third of Canada's rye whisky production. Extensive sections of the waterfront were filled in and the Don River was straightened, and soon the plant was nowhere near the lake. But with a railway siding beside the distillery, water transport was no longer needed.

In 1928 the firm merged with Hiram Walker of Windsor, and the Gooderham and Worts facility became a secondary production plant. In 1986 it was purchased by Allied Lyons of England. Four years later it was declared obsolete and closed. A century and a half of liquor production had ended.

Because it had been relegated to a lesser role in its later years, the entire complex was little altered, and remained much as it had appeared in the 1890s. Its size and age make it one of Canada's most remarkable historic industrial complexes, earning it recognition as a National Historic Site.

Still, for fifteen years the site sat vacant, although popular for movie shoots. Its brick streets and authentic facades provided set pieces for period movies such as *X-Men*, *The Hurricane* and the Academy Award-winning *Chicago*, as well as dozens of sketches in the television show *Kids in the Hall*. It is claimed that more than eight hundred movies and commercials have used the grounds for film sets.

In 2002, the entire complex was purchased by a group called Cityscape, which converted the two dozen buildings into a haven for artists and galleries, and in May of 2003, the "Distillery District" was formally opened. Various rooms, including the smoke house, the boiler house, the malting plant and the pure-spirits building, are now occupied by galleries, studios, bars and cafes, and where possible early machinery has been left in place. Despite inadequate public transit, tourists and Torontonians flock to the festivals and galleries such as the stunning Susan Ainslie glass gallery. Toronto's heritage planners have partly redeemed themselves with this industrial survivor.

The Gooderham and Worts industrial complex, a candidate for World Heritage designation.

25

The last Joy gas station is a relic from another era.

ODE TO JOY:
The Last Joy Gas Station

Architecture and gas stations just don't seem to go together. Mention the latter and one thinks of gas pumps, the smell of old oil and a building whose architecture is better left undiscussed.

But that wasn't the case during the 1920s and '30s, when the auto age was unfolding and gas stations were becoming part of the neighbourhood landscape. While price wars and gimmicks were the most common forms of competition, another method, undertaken first by the Hercules Oil Company of Detroit, was to create an attractive style of gas station.

Ironically, the style that Hercules chose was that which had been introduced more than thirty years earlier by the CPR when its railway stations were designed to attract passengers to the rail service. Known as the "chateau style," it incorporated steep bell-cast roofs and high towers. The Joy Oil Company introduced them to Toronto in 1937, and with their high red roofs and white stucco siding, these mini-chateaux soon became landmarks in many areas of the city. It is estimated that more than a dozen were built throughout Toronto.

Following the war, architectural styles changed. North America wanted to forget the hard years of war and the Depression that preceded it. Decorative features such as turrets and steep roofs were discarded in favour of the airiness and simplicity of flat roofs and large windows. Cars became bigger and soon clogged the streets and the growing network of highways, and to keep up, the gas stations needed to be larger and more efficient. The tiny Joy gas stations were inadequate to meet the economic and environmental needs of the new auto age. Corporate image was important too, and the subsequent owners of the Joy stations replaced them with the newest styles.

The old Joy stations quickly began to disappear from the landscape. By the mid-1980s only four remained in Toronto, and by 1992 there was just one. Located at the northwest corner of Lakeshore Boulevard West and Windermere Avenue, this solitary station was built while the Queen Elizabeth Way was under construction, which, until the Gardiner Expressway opened in the 1950s, connected directly to the lakeshore.

In 1989, the city of Toronto designated the unlikely little structure as a heritage building. In 2000, Olco, then the station's operator, finally closed the pumps and sold the site for affordable housing. Happily, plans for the housing units will incorporate the old gas station into the design, and so an unlikely and largely uncelebrated component of Toronto's heritage will survive.

A UTILITARIAN BEAUTY:
The R. C. Harris Filtration Plant

In the east end of Toronto, on a grassy slope overlooking Lake Ontario, sits one of the city's most attractive and least-known buildings—a filtration plant. Buildings housing public utilities seldom inspire either architectural elegance or public interest. But this one is different, and its difference is attributed to its namesake, Rowland Cole Harris.

Designed by Thomas Pomphrey, the building was constructed between 1932 and 1941. A second building was added in the early '50s. It was named after Harris, who was at the time Toronto's commissioner of works, and was a man who appreciated grand public buildings. The style that Harris chose for his filtration plant was Art Deco, an attractive modern style in vogue during the 1920s and '30s and often used for skyscrapers and other grand buildings of the day.

Characterized by streamlined curves and shapes, Art Deco is also a style that was relatively short-lived. After the Second World War, the tastes of a generation railed against the recent past, the years of war and Depression. Architects moved to a simpler form known simply as the International style.

The R. C. Harris Filtration Plant occupies an extensive grassy park. The older structure, closer to the lake, is the pumping station, which draws water from over 2 kilometres out in the lake, while the higher building does the filtering and chlorinating.

While sleek lines dominate the exterior, herringbone tiles of marble imported from Siena decorate the foyer and vast halls. In these halls the plant can process 175 million gallons of water each day. Like the Distillery District, the R. C. Harris plant is popular with film companies as a modernistic set for movies.

While the public is free to wander the grounds, tours of the interior were halted following the September 11, 2001, attacks on the World Trade Centre in New York. It was feared that a terrorist on such a tour might poison the city's water supply.

The plant is located on Queen Street East at Neville, the eastern terminus of the Queen Street streetcar line. It also marks the eastern end of the popular Toronto neighbourhood known as the Beaches, with its lakeside boardwalk and trendy cafes and stores.

The Art Deco R. C. Harris sewage treatment plant.

A TOUCH OF HOLLAND:
The Bayfield Windmill

A field of tall grass bends before the warm summer wind. Above the field, four huge wooden wind sails creak in a slow circle. They belong to North America's only wind-powered saw and grist mill. Located near the Lake Huron port village of Bayfield, it is known as the Folmar Windmill.

Frank de Jong is descended from generations of Dutch millers. Wind-powered sawmills, though rare in Canada, are part of his family heritage, and remained in his blood when he migrated to Canada following the Second World War. When he purchased a parcel of land beside the Bayfield River, southeast of Goderich, Ontario, he set about to recreate his own touch of Holland—a saw and grist mill that would be powered by wind alone. Eighteen years went into creating the mill pond on the Bayfield River, and thirteen into building the mill. Its design was based on an actual mill in Holland known as "the Arend."

When it was finished, the mill, wind cap and sails towered 29 metres above the Bayfield River marshlands. Although the mill remains privately owned, it is open to the public on a seasonal basis, and indeed has become one of the area's best-known attractions.

For a society accustomed to the ceaseless roar of cars and trucks, the only sounds here are the creaking of the sails. On the main floor of the mill, cables and hooks drag the logs up onto the slipway, where they are pulled slowly forward to the saw blades. These can number from two to twelve depending on the desired thickness of the cut lumber. Above the mill, a balcony encircles the wind cap. Above that are the four 22-metre wind sails, which rotate slowly in the wind.

When the mill is open, guides explain how the sails can be positioned to face the wind and how the rotation of the huge sails alone operates the saw and the grist mill. No longer a fully commercial operation, the mill now performs only custom jobs or for tourists. The entire area offers plenty to see, from the beautiful and busy tree-lined streets of Bayfield to the strange octagonal main street of Goderich, and the heritage park in the ghost town of St. Joseph.

The Folmar Mill is located south of Huron County Road 13 about 3 kilometres east of Highway 21. Look for the green arrows that point the way to Ontario's touch of Holland.

Bayfield's wind-powered sawmill.

CARVED IN STONE:
The Apple Park Farm Statues

If you stop to buy apple cider, apple butter or even plain old apples at the Apple Park Farm, don't be surprised if you get the feeling that you are being watched. Surrounding this attractive brick farmhouse on Highway 8 just east of Goderich are more than fifty stone figures that depict pioneer life in Ontario, or at least one man's view of it.

George Laithwaite moved to the farm from nearby Holmesville in 1895, and for the next sixty years carved from local limestone his depiction of the people and scenes that he saw around him. In pioneer Ontario, with no radio or TV shows to sap the imagination, reading the Bible was a popular pastime. Accordingly, Laithwaite drew from the scriptures scenes for his sculptures of a lion with a lamb and of the Queen of Sheba. He satirized politicians with his portrayal of Sir John A. Macdonald and Sir Robert Borden turning swords into ploughshares. The more raucous aspects of pioneer life appear in the caricatures of a drunken farmhand staggering home supported by his braying donkey, and in four drunken fishermen tottering home from a "fishing" trip.

Early travellers to Goderich soon began to go out of their way to see Laithwaite's sculptures, and at one point they were so popular that he sold postcards from his studio. Although Laithwaite died in 1956, the farm remains in the family. The statues are placed around a 3-acre lawn, while apples, apple cider and apple butter are produced from the 350 trees on the farm.

One of the more rollicking of the Park Farm statues.

THE HOLE IN THE HILL:
The Strange Story of the Eugenia Arches

Dry most of the year, and unknown to most Ontario travellers, Eugenia Falls in the Beaver Valley has been the site of some strange activities. In the 1850s, a case of mistaken identity led to a short-lived gold rush. Mistaking the shiny lustre of iron pyrite for gold, a pair of hunters sparked a flurry of digging and panning until the shine proved to be only fool's gold.

The next venture was more practical. In the 1870s, William Hogg from Hogg's Hollow, just north of Toronto, bought land adjacent to the falls and built a small electric plant to provide power to a few local communities. Buoyed by his success, Hogg went back to Toronto to try to sell city officials his power for their expanding streetcar system; however, the Adam Beck plant at Niagara Falls was closer and more reliable, so Toronto's politicians sent a dejected Hogg back to Eugenia.

In 1903 a group of Toronto businessmen formed the Georgian Bay Power Company and tried once again to capitalize on the questionable power potential of the falls. To maximize the drop, they excavated a tunnel through the hill beside the falls to the bottom of the valley far below. They began digging the tunnel in 1906, but unexpected problems with quicksand pushed the cost to over $1 million. Still, by 1907 the tunnel was finished. At 264 metres long, 2.7 metres high and 2.6 metres wide, it was big enough to drive a buggy through. And someone did just that.

Perhaps it was pride of workmanship, but the distinguishing features of the tunnel were the beautiful stone arches at either end, described by some as Roman in appearance. The plant never did operate, and the tunnel remained dry. Instead, a dam was built at Eugenia Lake itself, from which an even greater and more reliable fall of water could supply a larger plant built further down the Beaver Valley. For many years the wooden flumes remained a landmark in the Beaver Valley, but they have since been removed.

Although the tunnels themselves have long collapsed, the arches have withstood weathering and erosion. They are located in the Eugenia Falls Conservation Area, in the village of Eugenia, which lies on Grey County Road 13. The larger and more complete of the two arches stands near the brink of the falls on the opposite side of the river from the path and parking lot. (For safety reasons, the park authority discourages visitors from crossing the river above the falls.) The second arch, near the base of the hill, has collapsed and can only be found after a long and steep hike and a bit of luck.

The entrance to the long-lost tunnel at Eugenia.

POINT PELEE:
Where Canada Begins

Stand here and all of Canada is north of you. So, for that matter, is much of California. At 42 degrees north latitude, Point Pelee is the most southerly part of mainland Canada and lies south of much of the continental United States, including northern California. Such a southern latitude also provides the point with a range of southern vegetation found nowhere else in Ontario, vegetation more common, in fact, to the Carolinas. Even prickly pear cactus is found here. Indeed, the rare plant and animal life has earned the point its status as one of Canada's first national parks.

But its history goes back far beyond that. Owing to Point Pelee's strategic location, well into Lake Erie and close to American shipping lanes, the British military in the 1790s set the point aside as a naval reserve. That didn't stop a handful of squatters, known as "Pointers," from moving in and starting up fishing and small-time farming.

The sandy soil limited the range of crops, and the point gradually became more popular with hunters and birdwatchers. Then, in 1918, through the efforts of ornithologist Percy Taverner and his bird-lover friend Jack Miner (founder of the nearby Jack Miner Bird Sanctuary), the government of Canada designated the reserve as a national park, one of Canada's first.

Commercial fishing operations persisted until the last lease expired in 1969, and a few cottagers hung around even after that. Nature lovers now arrive from around the world to enjoy the rare plants and animals, but especially the spectacular fall migration of the beautiful monarch butterfly, during which branches of trees are entirely enveloped in the orange-and-black creatures.

Park planners have made the park's many features easy to see. Boardwalks guide nature lovers through the vast marshes, and pathways lead them to the cactus patch. Even one of the old squatter shacks has been preserved for history buffs.

But the most unusual experience in the park is the point itself. After the trees end, a bare sand spit leads another 1.25 kilometres into the lake. (This, some believe, gave the point its name, the word Pelee meaning "bald," or "peeled," in French.) The point narrows until it becomes a pencil point and then fades into waves. But you can walk beyond even that into the shallow waters of Lake Erie and look back on Canada—all of it.

Point Pelee is Canada's most southerly point of land.

THE TELLTALE GRAVE:
The Donnelly Tombstone

It's okay to go to Lucan these days and talk about the Donnellys, a topic which, a few short years ago, would result in cold stares or an even more severe rebuke. But a century ago all of North America was talking about the "Black Donnellys" and their untimely demise.

On a bitterly cold night in February 1880, a local vigilante gang attacked two homes belonging to a family of Irish immigrants named the Donnellys, and brutally butchered five of their number. Members of several prominent local families stood accused of the gristly slaughter, among them the sheriff, and a horrified world followed the macabre details in the newspapers.

Daily newspaper reports of the trial kept the English-speaking world transfixed for months. The first trial resulted in a hung jury. In the second, the judge, allegedly following instructions from his political masters who were seeking re-election, ordered the jury to disregard the testimony of a youthful witness, and the vigilantes went free.

The massacre was the result of an ancient Irish feud and a bitter business rivalry, all played out in an era when drunkenness and violence were part of pioneer life. Eventually the feud reached such a fever pitch that beatings and burnings became routine, and many of them were blamed on the large Donnelly clan.

Lucan is one of those down-to-earth towns where many residents can still trace their roots back to the first pioneers. Several had grandparents or great-grandparents who were part of the simmering feud, and even a few who were part of the mob. Today time, and perhaps celebrity, have combined to ease, if not altogether erase, the bitterness. The local museum recounts the tragedy, while the current owner of the homestead property hosts group tours (by appointment only), vividly re-enacting the events of that deadly night. The house on the site now was built by one of the surviving sons after the original cabin crashed in flames the night of the murders, marked only by stones laid at the cabin's four corners.

The "Swamp Schoolhouse" where the vigilantes hatched their plot still stands, used now as storage shed. But the strongest reminder of that night lies in the graveyard of St. Patrick's Roman Catholic Church, the very church where the sworn enemies had even worshipped together. That reminder is the marble headstone listing all the names of the family members who were cut down that night.

The original marker, now secreted away in a northern Ontario basement, used the word "murdered" to describe their demise, but vandalism forced its removal. Today's stone says simply "died." The graveyard lies at the corner of Highway 4 and the Roman Line, about 25 kilometres north of London, Ontario. The homestead itself is about 6 kilometres north of that.

Since the tale of the feud first resurfaced in the early 1950s in a book called *The Black Donnellys*, some six fiction and fourteen nonfiction books have been published on the horrific crime. It obviously remains hard not to talk about it these days, even in Lucan.

The Donnelly tombstone still sees many visitors.

GOING AROUND IN CIRCLES:
Goderich's Eight-Sided Main Street

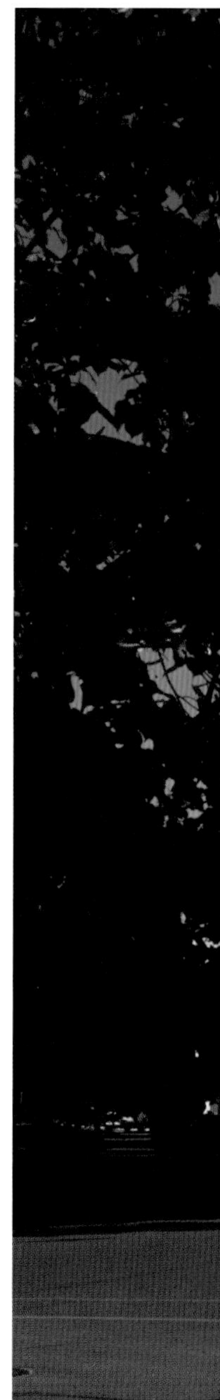

If you spend any time driving on Goderich's main street, you soon get the sense that you've been going around in circles. Goderich has an unusual main street. Designed to accommodate the convergence of eight radiating streets onto a market square, it is a perfect octagon.

It was chosen by John Galt, the first commissioner of the Canada Company, a pioneer land settlement company, who wanted the town that was his headquarters to be unique. Drawing on the city planning concepts of Roman architect Marcus Pollio Vitruvius, he laid his eight-sided town down in the uncleared forests of pioneer Ontario. Few other examples of the style exist anywhere in the world, and none are as exact as that in Goderich.

With the arrival of the Buffalo, Brantford and Goderich Railway in 1858, and the Guelph and Goderich Railway in 1908, the town boomed. A grand courthouse replaced the market in the centre of the square, and hotels and stores of yellow brick filled in the eight sides.

Although some have been lost to redevelopment, a number of the more outstanding buildings have survived. One of the most imposing is the three-storey Bedford Hotel, built in 1896 and located between South and Kingston streets, and recently renovated. With its corner entrance and its magnificent domed roof, it visually dominates that side of the square. Near the corner of Kingston Street stands the former Victoria Opera House. Built in 1887, it is characterized by high, arching windows on the second and third storeys.

The original courthouse burned in 1948 and was replaced by a more modern building. With funds from the Ontario government, the town and the business community have improved and upgraded the appearance of the square with brick sidewalks, new streetlights, benches and planters.

Goderich has more to offer the heritage enthusiast than just the square. The unusual octagonal jailhouse, located north of the square on Victoria Street, is now a museum. West Street leads to the lake and takes you past the Port of Goderich town hall. Once at the lake, you see the former CPR railway station with its strange-looking "witch's hat" roof above what was the waiting room. The CPR has removed its tracks, and the building is now owned by the municipality.

Another one-time railway station sits four blocks east of the square at the corner of East and Maitland. This former CNR station, with its two attractive towers, has been recently sold to private owners who are committed to its restoration.

Goderich does indeed have much to offer visitors, once they stop going around in circles and figure out how to get off that darned eight-sided main street!

Goderich's eight-sided main street was based on an early Roman town plan by architect Marcus Pollio Vitruvius.

The log White Otter Castle was built by one man alone in the bush.

THE LOG CASTLE ON WHITE OTTER LAKE

Those things that are the hardest to reach often offer the richest rewards. So is the case with the strange log castle on White Otter Lake, some 64 kilometres north of Atikokan, in northwestern Ontario. Accessible only by boat, float plane or four-wheel drive, this three-storey mansion was constructed entirely of red pine logs by a wiry little man only 5 foot 7 inches, with no help and no machinery.

In 1887, James McQuat arrived from Scotland to carve out a farm in the wilderness of northwestern Ontario. A decade of inconsistent crops followed. Then came the cry "gold!" The northwestern Ontario gold rush was on, and McQuat joined the stampede into the bush. But he fared no better at prospecting than he had at farming. Determined to show his worth to society and, it is said, to attract the love of a lady, McQuat decided to build a castle. He chose a sand beach on the northwest arm of White Otter Lake. Here, facing west, he could enjoy his favourite image, the spectacular northwestern sunset.

He carefully chose the finest logs, hand winched them through the bush, squared them on three sides, and carefully dovetailed the ends to make an airtight fit. By using skids, holes and pegs, McQuat patiently and painstakingly inched the logs up the walls, until finally his tower stood four storeys high and measured more than 3 metres square at the base. The main house was three storeys high and 7 metres square, while a further two-storey addition at the back served as his living quarters.

Contrary to later legend, McQuat was neither a hermit nor an eccentric. Rather, he enjoyed company and travelled frequently to the busy railway town of Ignace, the nearest supply point, and often showed off photographs of his home.

The irony was that his castle was never his own, for he had squatted on Crown land. For three years he carried on a futile effort to acquire the title, but the Department of Lands and Forests, unimpressed by his remarkable feat, repeatedly denied his requests. His dispute abruptly ended when on October 8, 1920, he become entangled in his fishing nets only metres away from his castle and drowned. He was fifty-eight years old.

For seven decades his castle has stood empty, damaged by water but generally free from vandals. In 1955 the department added concrete foundations, new roofing and better bracing. It was later more fully restored by the Friends of White Otter.

You can reach White Otter Castle from a number of fishing camps on the lake, or by boat from Clearwater Lake on Highway 622. And as you watch the sun set over the quiet, northern lake, you will understand why Jimmy McQuat called it home.

GRAND CANYON NORTH:
Ouimet Canyon

It's little wonder that Group of Seven painters A. Y. Jackson, Franklin Carmichael and Lauren Harris fell in love with Superior country. Nearly every bend in its rivers and nearly every bay in its lakes displays a panorama of mountain scenery that is as unexpected as it is awesome. And when, at the end of a trail through a pine forest near Nipigon, Ontario, the land drops away, unannounced, at your feet, to reveal a sudden and magnificent canyon, you understand how scenery can be called "unexpected."

As a tourist attraction, Ouimet Canyon Provincial Park is relatively unknown. No motels have sprung up to accommodate the hoards, no gift shops line the roads. Most Trans-Canada Highway travellers simply ignore the simple brown sign that points the way. But as a visual spectacle, Ouimet Canyon is breathtaking and unique.

The craggy crevice, 150 metres wide and 100 deep, twists several kilometres north from the lip of the grand plateau into which it has been cut. So little sunshine penetrates the deep gully that winter ice can linger into summer, and only hardy Arctic species of mosses, lichens and liverworts can survive.

The canyon traces its origins back to the last great ice age, when glaciers 2 kilometres thick crept southward, scouring and gouging everything in their path. Here at Ouimet Canyon, a tongue of ice crept down what was an eroded diabase sill. That diabase was formed a billion years ago when magma rose to the surface, creating the pillar-like formations that line the valley walls. Some of those pillars, due to erosion, are free-standing.

The road to Ouimet Canyon from the Trans-Canada Highway (about 55 kilometres east of Thunder Bay) passes some surprisingly lush farmland before twisting its way up the face of the rocky plateau. From the parking lot in the provincial park an easy trail winds through the forest for about a kilometre up to the sudden and unfenced rim of the canyon. If you fear heights, or worry about small kids, designated viewing areas do have guardrails around them. There are longer and more difficult trails that lead the hiker into the depths of the gorge.

From the viewing areas, the panorama encompasses not only the defile itself but also its rugged gates at the rim of the plateau, the forested lands beyond, and along the far horizon the grey waters of Lake Superior.

As you gaze at the results of nature's remarkable strength, as the northern stillness rings in your ears, and as the sharp, pine-scented air stings your nostrils, you will understand why the Group of Seven kept coming back.

Ontario's miniature version of the Grand Canyon, Ouimet Canyon, is so deep and narrow that plants otherwise native to the Arctic thrive in its dark recesses.

COBALT'S BOOM-TOWN LEGACY

When a pair of railway timber scouts named McKinley and Darraugh discovered silver by a remote lake in northeastern Ontario in 1903, they couldn't have known that their find would change forever the landscape that surrounded them.

Shortly after the rails of the Temiscaming and Northern Ontario Railway reached the shores of that lake, a confusion of shacks and boom-town stores began to vie for space on the tumble of rock beside it. The railway called its station Cobalt (after the parent material, which contained the precious silver).

Almost overnight, the forest vanished as miners clanged into the granite, frantically grasping for the silver. And they weren't disappointed. From the bedrock came boulders of silver the size of sheds and veins the width of sidewalks. The trees were replaced by a forest of headframes that, at the peak of activity, numbered fifty-two. Cobalt boomed so quickly that there was no time for town planning. Streets ended abruptly at rock ridges, upon which a tumble of shacks, hotels and wooden stores were thrown together, while beneath the dusty streets half a dozen mines burrowed out a maze of shafts.

Between 1908 and 1910, the name Cobalt echoed around the world, and the town quickly grew to ten thousand. But the great Stock Market Crash of 1929 devastated the silver market, by which time many of the small deposits were depleted, and Cobalt became a ghost town.

Although Cobalt's population has rebounded to two thousand, you can find among the now-silent hills the ghosts of its heyday. Simply follow the well-marked Heritage Silver Trail at the western entrance to the town (Highway 11B). This trail will guide you to gaping fissures that once contained the fabulous silver veins, and past the ghostly forest of headframes.

These mines are still now, their rusting headframes guarding both the western and eastern approaches to the town. But in the centre of the one-time boom town stands the most unusual sight of all, a headframe protruding from the roof of a store. When the Coniagas Mine ceased operating in 1926, Anthony Ciachino built a store around the shaft and used the cool air from its depths to refrigerate his meat and vegetables. The store operated until the 1960s, when the Cobalt Area Restoration Office took it over.

Perhaps Cobalt's grandest building was its unusual station. To complement Cobalt's new status as the cultural centre of New Ontario, the railway commissioned John Lyle to design a station that would show off the railway to the world. Completed in 1909, the station was the finest on the line and one of the most elegant in Ontario. With its Beaux-Art lines and arched, two-storey facade, the station was one of the town's most interesting buildings, and one of the few made of brick. Following its closure the station sat empty until it was converted into a military museum.

Cobalt is unusually rich in its boom-town heritage, with the Fred Larose blacksmith shop

(Larose found one of the town's richest deposits when, legend says, he threw a pickaxe at a fox), its narrow streets and Ontario's first provincial police lockup. Sadly, however, much has been lost to fires and demolition.

The local mining museum provides walking tours of the town's heritage sites, as well as a driving tour of the headframes and a guided tour of a former mine shaft. In 2002, TVOntario's television program Studio 2 awarded the town the status of being "Ontario's Most Historic Town."

A Cobalt grocer built his store around an abandoned headframe to keep his meat and produce cool.

36

Tourists crowd onto the local train in the heart of the scenic Agawa Canyon.

THE ALGOMA CENTRAL:
A Train Ride from the Past

As the first rays of sunrise brighten the streets of Hearst, bleary-eyed tourists begin to wander to the platform of the Algoma Central Railway (ACR) station. Awaiting them on the tracks are the two passenger cars of ACR's Train 632, also known as the "Milk Run." They are about to embark on one of the last of the old-style train rides in Canada.

Not a museum train, 632 is all utilitarian. The 476-kilometre line between the sleepy sawmill town of Hearst and the bustling industrial city of Sault Ste. Marie is populated by prospectors, loggers, trappers, cottagers and campers, all dependent upon this train to link them with the "outside."

Throughout the ride, the train often stops on demand. At Wabatong, a wooden "umbrella" station beside Wabatong Lake, cottagers and fishermen climb on board. At Oba, a community of one hundred still entirely dependent on rail access, parcels and freight are hand loaded on or off the mail car, while the passengers scurry into the nearby store for a coffee. Oba is the railway's junction with Canadian National Railway's main line, and its stuccoed two-storey station, built by the Canadian Northern Railway, testifies to this status, although its rundown condition shows its new owners' lack of interest in that heritage. Further down the line, another rail-dependent village, Franz, now nearly a ghost town, is the ACR's junction with the CPR.

The morning hours of the southbound are spent hurtling through a low spruce forest that is flat and dreary, but includes the "floating" bridges of Oba Lake, built on pilings driven into the seemingly bottomless muskeg. Later, during the afternoon, spectacular cliffs loom above a foaming stream as the train enters the Agawa Canyon. This ancient and spectacular defile is the destination of the internationally popular tourist trains, the longest in the world, that depart daily from Sault Ste. Marie. But unlike the tourist trains, the Milk Run does not stop to allow for an afternoon of picnicking and hiking.

Throughout the trip, which can last up to ten hours, an easy joviality permeates the train. Tourists gape at the passing landscape, while cottagers, campers and canoists scramble on at the many flag stops, as acquaintances are renewed and familiar chatter fills the coaches. Finally the train hisses to a halt at the modern Sault station. Last farewells are heard, and the empty train eases away from the platform to await the morning run.

(Two economical alternatives to the tour train include the "Canyon Combo," which places passengers on the northbound tour train at 8:00 a.m. with a transfer onto the southbound local train at the Agawa Canyon station. The other is to drive to the Frater station, located east of the Trans-Canada Highway, for the 12-kilometre trip on the 12:55 p.m. local train to the canyon, there to await the 14:20 p.m. southbound local back to Frater. This can only be done on a Saturday or Sunday.)

THE WHITE CRESTS OF KILLARNEY

Driving west on Highway 637, just south of Sudbury, you soon see the domes of white, gleaming above the low, green forest. Your first thoughts are that freak weather has preserved a mountain of snow into the summer season. But as you drive closer you realize that these are the legendary La Cloche Mountains of Killarney, and the "snow" is quartzite rock of pure white.

About two billion years ago an ancient sea laid down a bed of sand that was unusually rich in silica. As the shifting bedrock hurled the seabed into a giant mountain range, the layers of silica were compressed into masses of white quartzite, forming a mountain range loftier than today's Rockies. Eons of rain, wind and grinding glaciers eroded the peaks into the round, white knobs that today provide the spectacular backdrop for the northern shores of Georgian Bay and Lake Huron. The white wall of mountains stretches in a thin line for about 60 kilometres and soars in places to heights of 500 metres.

The early French explorers gave the mountains their word for "bell," because they reported that certain rocks, when struck, echoed like a bell.

The area's early history has little to do with the scenery. Following the days when Killarney was a stopover for Native and French-Canadian fur traders, logging companies began to strip the pine from the mountainsides. The village of Killarney, now dependent upon tourism, originated as a fur-trading post and fishing village.

But it was the scenery that attracted the area's earliest tourists. Among them were a pair of young painters named Franklin Carmichael and A. Y. Jackson, whose works *Summer Storm*, *Bay of Islands*, and *Nellie Lake* have become among the most prized Group of Seven works. Their works in part inspired the Ontario government to create the much-visited Killarney Provincial Park, with its campsites, canoe routes and hiking trails, one of which is 100 kilometres long.

The park is 70 kilometres west of Highway 69 along Highway 637.

You can also travel by boat to Killarney and explore the mountain-lined fjords. Or you can approach the mountains on Highway 6 south of Espanola to a soaring pass over the Tower Mountain summit near Willisville. But regardless of how you get there, the La Cloche Mountains of Killarney remain one of the most unusual alpine destinations east of the Rockies.

The pure white quartzite rocks of the Killarney mountains resemble a hillside of snow.

SUDBURY'S LITTLE ITALY

Most Ontario towns and villages tend to resemble each other. Their roads were surveyed into standard widths of 33 or 66 feet, while residential lots were laid out in uniform grids. But tucked away in the former town of Copper Cliff, a company town constructed by the Canada Copper Company (later Inco), lies a hillside of houses, crammed together and jostling for position, reminiscent of an Italian mountainside community. And the reason is simple—that's what it is.

In 1883, the construction of the Canadian Pacific Railway unearthed deposits of copper and nickel in a massive geological basin. Headframes, mills and smelter stacks began to appear on the rocky hilltops, turning a railway town known as Sudbury Junction into one of the world's greatest mining centres.

The first was the Murray Mine, followed by Falconbridge and then Copper Cliff. To avoid paying heavy local taxes, the companies built their own towns, and in 1880, Copper Cliff was laid out by the Canada Copper Company. Here, west of Sudbury, beneath the looming smelter, the company laid out wide streets and built stores, a hospital, a club and neat company houses.

But on a vacant hilltop, mere metres from the belching chimneys, a group of Italian miners decided to build their own houses, and petitioned for a parcel of land from the company. With no preplanned streets or lots to follow, they built in the rural Italian style to which they were accustomed. Their strong sense of community meant that proximity to each other outweighed the desire for privacy or large lots. They built their houses in whatever shape, size or orientation suited them. Little space was left for yards, even less for streets, for at the time none owned cars.

The result is a scene almost from an Italian postcard. Narrow streets twist around the houses, which squeeze each other at every angle. Although the homes are individually owned, the area has remained resolutely Italian—Italian clubs and language dominate. Only metres from the nearest houses, Inco's refinery stacks soar into the sky. The stacks have been a symbol that once turned many away from the area, but seventy years ago the smelter meant jobs for a community of Italian miners and drew them, almost as if in reverence, to huddle at its feet.

Taste of the Appenines. Little Italy, an Italian enclave within Sudbury's Copper Cliff townsite, was built by Italian migrant miners to resemble their native mountainside villages.

39

STONEHENGE ONTARIO?

While the unusual aggregation of eighteen huge boulders, some twice the height of a person, in the bushland on the north shore of Larder Lake may not replicate the dramatic visual impact of the Stonehenge formation on England's stark Salisbury Plain, its strange alignments do raise some questions.

How did the giant boulders get there? There are simply too many of them in a small area, 2 hectares, for the great glaciers to have randomly deposited them. And why do their alignments match exactly with the rising and setting of the sun on the summer and winter solstices? And can their proximity to Mt. Cheminis, a huge volcanic plug that dominates the landscape 20 kilometres to the east, and which was once a Native shrine, be simply a coincidence?

Perhaps one of the clues lies in the most recent interpretation of the de Troyes diary. Pierre de Troyes was a French soldier who in 1686 travelled overland from the St. Lawrence River to surprise the British garrison at Moose Fort, on James Bay. To make his way through the unfamiliar Ontario bushland, de Troyes followed ancient Native routes. A recent reinterpretation of his diary places the main route not to the east, as previously assumed, but along Larder Lake, and right past the mystery boulders.

Other clues include results of nearby archaeological digs that place the Natives' presence at more than six thousand years ago. And a field of jagged rocks may represent an ancient Native quarry that lies nearby. Together, the clues point to the possibility that here in northeastern Ontario lies a major and hitherto undetected centre of Native worship. Because the boulders have so long been hidden by the bush and their alignments never before taken, archaeologists have only recently begun to investigate. Are they truly another "Stonehenge," or simply a random arrangement?

Because the rocks must be protected from interference until security is established, those who wish to visit the site should inquire locally in the town of Larder Lake for directions.

Four bolders in a line on the shore of Larder Lake.

THE RUINS OF ST. RAPHAEL

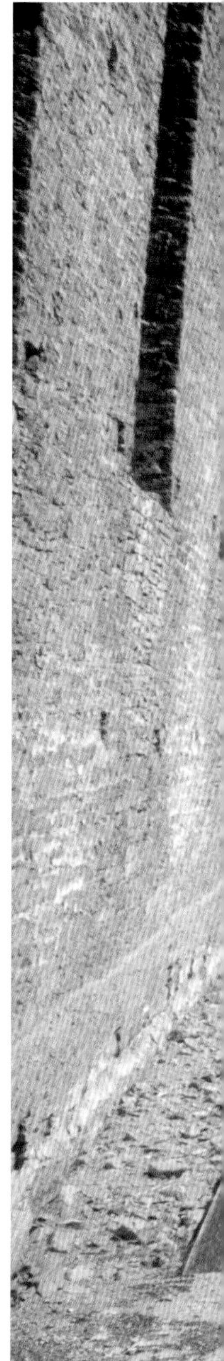

Ruins, romantic and picturesque, are more associated with Europe than with North America. Here, ruins tend to be of factories and mills, harsh forms that reflect our obsession with industry rather than beauty. But the ruins of the magnificent St. Raphael Cathedral on County Road 18, 40 kilometres northeast of Cornwall, contain a history, romance and grace that one would more closely identify with Greece or Rome.

In 1764, the revolutionary war in the United States was over, and in return for their loyalty and courage, those who fought for England were rewarded with land grants in what would become Ontario. After trooping wearily behind their commander, Sir John Johnson, the officers and men of the 1st Battalion, King's Royal Regiment of New York (most of Highland Scots origin), finally arrived on the banks of the Raisin River. Here, in eastern Ontario's Charlottenburg Township, their land grants, swampy and forested, awaited them.

Two years later, five hundred more Scots arrived direct from the highlands, led by their parish priest, Alexander Macdonnell. The parish grew and prospered. The first father Macdonnell died in 1803 and was replaced by another priest of the same name. The second Father Macdonnell succeeded in making his parish, which he called St. Raphael, the administrative centre of the Catholic Church in Upper Canada.

In 1815 he ordered the building of a large stone church on a hilltop overlooking the farms of his flock. In 1821 the church was consecrated, and when the priest was appointed bishop, the church became a cathedral. It was the largest church in Upper Canada. Five years later he added the Iona Seminary.

For a century and a half, the cathedral dominated the rolling farmlands from its hilltop perch. Then, in 1970, fire roared through the structure. Flames lashed out through the windows, as the roof collapsed in a whirl of sparks. But again the tenacity of their roots came to the fore, bolstered now by the infusion of French-Canadian Catholics, and the parishioners decided the ruins should be neither demolished nor replaced, but rather remain a ruin.

Now landscaped, and under the stewardship of the Friends of St. Raphael, the ruins remain the focus of the parish. Services and plays now occur under a roofless sky, while the Friends continue to try and raise funds to maintain the structure. Although the Ontario Heritage Foundation has designated the building, it provides no financial aid.

The picturesque ruins of St. Raphael Cathedral.

ONTARIO'S SMALLEST FERRY

As Ontarians hurl their cars along the expressways and toll roads, few pause to consider the more leisurely pace of a ferry ride. Many have tried the popular MS *Chi-Cheemaun*, which swallows 115 cars at a time and glides them across Georgian Bay to and from Manitoulin Island. Few, however, realize that Ontario claims no fewer than sixteen car ferry services, nearly all of them free. Three car ferries cross each of the Ottawa and St. Clair rivers, a pair are for island Native reserves, while Canada's southernmost ferry links mainland Ontario with Pelee Island, Canada's most southerly occupied island. But the greatest concentration of ferries lies near Kingston.

Here, at the entrance to the St. Lawrence River, a handful of large, flat islands attracted early pioneer settlers. Although the populations have subsequently declined, the islands remain occupied, the ferries their lifeline to the mainland.

The largest of the five, the *Wolfe Islander III*, carries more than fifty cars and trucks to busy Wolfe Island. While others link Howe Island and Amherst Island to the mainland, the smallest of them all is the three-car ferry to Simcoe Island. Announced only by a small sign, the landing is nothing more than a beach. Here, the little ferry grinds against the sand and unceremoniously plunks down its gangway. Because it links Simcoe Island only to Wolfe Island, and not to the mainland, the ferry coincides its schedule with that of the *Wolfe Islander III*, or runs as required.

Once home to more than a dozen farm families, Simcoe Island is now more popular for cottaging, and only a pair of farms survive. At the far western end of the limestone island stands the historic Nine-Mile Point Lighthouse. Now automated, the 15-metre tower dates from 1833, and is popular with lighthouse enthusiasts, although it is surrounded by privately owned land. Although it is only one of sixteen ferries that ply Ontario's water, the Simcoe Island ferry is the smallest, and takes you on an unusual excursion to a place where cars are an anomaly rather than the norm.

The Simcoe Island ferry is one of Ontario's smallest and least-known ferry services.

THE LAKE ON THE MOUNTAIN

At first it looks natural enough—a little lake sparkling in the sun, surrounded by willow trees. But you look behind you, and 100 metres below, at the foot of a limestone cliff, spreads Lake Ontario's Bay of Quinte. Then it begins to sink in. The little lake beside you is sitting on the brink of a cliff, with no visible outlet and no visible source.

Located in Prince Edward County, 7 kilometres from the town of Picton, the lake has long puzzled geologists. How did get there? Why has it stayed there? Until just a few years ago no one even knew how deep it was. Then, as they explored its depths, geologists determined that it was spring fed and about 60 metres deep. But just as they were solving these puzzles, the scientists uncovered another even more intriguing mystery. The fluctuations in the water level of the lake seemed to coincide with those occurring in Lake Erie, more than 100 kilometres away and with no direct connection.

Its origins, too, have defied explanation. While most theories involving glacial whirlpools, meteors, and volcanoes have been dismissed, the one most commonly accepted involves the collapse of a massive limestone cave beneath the surface. The early Indians believed it was the lake of the gods, and called it Onokenoga.

The attractions around the lake are numerous and don't have a lot to do with its mysteries. A small provincial park beside the lake provides picnicking and hiking, while across the road a lofty viewpoint offers vistas of the Bay of Quinte, the mainland shore, and the free Glenora ferries that shuttle back and forth carrying Highway 33 traffic.

Van Alstine's stone store, which dates from the days of the Loyalists, sits beside the park, while at the foot of the cliff the several buildings that comprise the Glenora mill complex are among the oldest stone mill buildings in the province. But all attention focusses upon the Lake on the Mountain. It has been a mystery since it was discovered, and it will likely remain a mystery for some time to came.

Picton's mysterious Lake on the Mountain lurks near the lip of the cliff that overlooks the Glenora mill.

THE DUNE THAT ATE A TOWN

Although it didn't exactly "eat" a town, a giant wall of sand did move across Prince Edward County between 1890 and 1920 to consume a sizeable settlement before finally being halted. And it was all due to beer.

The Civil War that tore apart the United States during the early 1860s had considerable impact on Canada. When the U.S. government slapped a surtax on whisky, American consumers switched to beer. And the best barley for beer was considered to be Canadian. Canadian farmers hurriedly turned all available fields to barley production. But Prince Edward County, with its mild climate and close proximity to U.S. ports just across Lake Ontario, became Ontario's major barley exporter. Cattle were hustled off their pastures and onto the most marginal lands in the county, the dunes.

Following the retreat of the last glaciers, the Prince Edward Peninsula acted to block Lake Ontario's eastward currents and built up a long beach of sand. Over the centuries the prevailing winds whipped the sand into a ridge of dunes that measured 8 kilometres long, 2 kilometres wide and 50 metres high. Over time, a matte of grasses and shrubs had stabilized the dunes. But once the cattle started to roam them, eating the fragile cover, the dunes grew restless and started once more to move.

Slowly at first, then with increasing determination, the dunes moved inland. Fields, fences and then outbuildings and barns soon disappeared under the moving yellow wall. The West Bay Road had to be realigned a number of times to avoid being consumed. The advancing dunes spared nothing. A brick factory stood stubbornly in the way of the dunes until wind-whipped sand finally forced the owners to dismantle the plant and flee. Even the Evergreen Lodge failed to withstand the onslaught and was also dismantled.

Desperate, the farmers planted willows on the dunes, but those had little effect. Finally, after the First World War had ended, a reluctant Ontario government established a tree nursery on them. As roots and branches grabbed the blowing sand the dunes slowed, but they haven't stopped.

Today, on the south shore of West Lake, both in and near the popular Sandbanks Provincial Park, you can see the advancing dunes. Cedar trees, once buried and now exposed, show double sets of roots, while relics of the pioneer brick factory still litter its ill-fated site. Although the dunes no longer advance across the countryside, the winds continue to whip the sand into West Lake. Eventually, the dunes that ate a sizeable settlement will claim the lake and turn it into little more than a pond. Their appetite is insatiable.

Dunes at West Lake.

WATERWAY FROM THE PAST:
The Rideau Canal

In 1826, the Duke of Wellington was a legend, hero of a determined campaign against another hero, Napoleon Bonaparte. His Peninsular Campaign done, Wellington's military mind looked to Upper Canada, where memories of the 1812 war with the Americans were still fresh. Wary that the major transportation corridor, the St. Lawrence, lay perilously close to the U.S. border (in part it forms the border), Wellington proposed a canal that would link Kingston, on Lake Ontario, with Wright's Town (now Hull), then a small sawmill village on the north side of the Ottawa River, a remote location well away from possible American actions.

To carry out the difficult job he coaxed his former co-campaigner, Colonel John By, out of retirement. For five years, two thousand men sweated in eastern Ontario's malarial swamplands, hacking bush, trenching channels, and hauling huge limestone blocks for the fifty dams and forty-seven locks. The accomplishment took a deadly toll, with an estimated death rate from malaria of more than 50 percent.

In 1832, By's 200-kilometre waterway opened for traffic, a remarkable feat given the remoteness and total lack of mechanical assistance. A small sawmill town sprang up at the canal's eastern terminus and was named Bytown, after the canal's builder. But By did not return home a hero. Instead, he was court-martialled for allowing his £577,000 budget to swell to more than £870,000. Not only that, but the Americans remained benign and the canal never fulfilled its military role.

However, prior to the railways it provided a key commercial link for the many little mill towns along its path. Then, with the arrival of the railway its use faded, not rising again until the 1950s and '60s, when the popularity of recreational boating boomed. During that time, in 1932, the federal government proposed closing the historic waterway. It was saved only by its role as a vital water-control system.

The canal is famed not just for its pleasure-boating, but for the fact that it remains historically intact, right down to the hand operation of its locks and swing bridges. In fact, in a rare gesture of heritage preservation, the federal government placed the canal's operation in the hands of Parks Canada and has identified the route as a historical monument.

By's military blockhouses still stand at Kingston Mills, Newboro and Merrickville. At Jones Falls are a triple set of locks, a one-time powder magazine and the world's highest stone dam of its day. The Scottish stonemasons who toiled to construct the stone walls and locks have also left a lasting legacy in the beautiful stone stores and homes of Perth, Merrickville and Kingston. Colonel By may have died a broken man, but even he would have been astonished at the durability of his legacy.

Colonel John By built these triple locks at Jones Falls when eastern Ontario was little more than a malarial swamp.

45

THE TEACHING ROCKS:
Peterborough's Petroglyphs

The hollow echo of water gurgling beneath the rocks at their feet made the two young geologists uneasy. There, in the stillness of the forest north of Stony Lake, they felt as though they had entered a hallowed place. As they swept away the moss from the white crystalline rocks, something caught their eye. Something odd. The surface of the rock was not smooth, as it should have been. Rather, it contained strange etchings, more than nine hundred of them. Although they did not know it on that day in May 1954, the two men had uncovered one of North America's largest and most mysterious Native petroglyphs, the Teaching Rocks.

Like the Christian Bible, the Teaching Rocks tell the Aboriginal story of life. As each young male entered adolescence, the elders of the tribe would lead him to the site, guided by the sound of waterfalls and special guide rocks. One lesson at a time, the elders taught the youngsters the meaning of life, as the Ojibway understood it and as the Teaching Rocks revealed it. The medicine wheel told them that life began as the sunrise in the east. Midday represented midlife, and the west meant old age, while the north referred to the afterlife. The spirits portrayed in the carvings taught that man must coexist with nature.

After each lesson finished, the elders would cover the stones with moss to preserve the carvings from erosion. In 1976, the site, sacred to the First Nations, became a provincial park under the cooperative stewardship of the Curve Lake First Nation. A decade later, to protect the surface from the elements, a glass enclosure was added.

The site is located 55 kilometres northeast of Peterborough, near Highway 28. Here, you wonder at the strange shapes and possibly apply your own interpretations. Then you can watch the Ministry of Natural Resources's twenty-minute award-winning film, *The Teaching Rocks*. Prepared by Lloyd Walton, the film reveals the mysteries as told and narrated by the Ojibway themselves. As you walk back to your car through the woods, you look around you and see nature through different eyes, those of its original stewards.

The mysteries of the Native etchings in Petroglyph Provincial Park have recently been solved, in an award-winning movie, *The Teaching Rocks*, produced by Ontario's Ministry of Natural Resources.

BOATS IN THE AIR:
The Kirkfield Lift Lock

Snaking through the middle of Ontario is a water highway, a chain of lakes linked by short streams that connect Lake Ontario on the east and Georgian Bay on the west. Its name is familiar to most Ontarians as the Trent-Severn Waterway. To Ontario's early pioneers it was their lifeline—their only highway. Along its lakes, especially the Kawarthas, they floated out their logs, took their wheat to the mill, and travelled for their food.

Although the isolated settlers cried for canals to link the lakes and rivers as early as the 1820s, governments did not act until 1842, when the first lock was constructed at Bobcaygeon. By 1892 a system of locks and canals was nearly complete. But at Peterborough and Kirkfield the level of the water fell so sharply that four costly and water-consuming locks would be required at each location. For a solution, the engineers at Montreal's Dominion Bridge Company, contractor for the canal, looked to an insignificant village in England named Weaver Creek.

There, the locks on the canal were operated by an unusual system known as hydraulic lift locks. Two watertight boxes, each big enough to hold a boat, were balanced hydraulically side by side. As the upper box filled, it became heavier than the lower box and descended, forcing the lower box to the upper level as the lower box opened to release the cargo. This in turn made the lower container lighter and the positions changed. Savings over traditional locks both in time and construction costs, and especially in water usage, were enormous.

Built between 1896 and 1907, two such lift locks groaned into operation at Peterborough and Kirkfield, as Ontario watched in awe. The larger of the two, at Peterborough, looms 20 metres in the air, while that at Kirkfield measures about 17 metres. Each lock contains 1,700 tons of water. The two remain the largest in the world, and are the only examples of their kind in North America.

But they were too late to help the settlers. By then the countless little railway companies had created a dense network of railway lines that made water transportation obsolete.

Today, recreation remains the sole function of the Trent Canal and its lift locks. To reflect this emphasis, the whole Trent Canal system is run by the federal department responsible for recreation, Parks Canada. Even for landlubbers the sight a bucket of boats high in the air has become a tourist attraction in its own right. The lock at Kirkfield is accessible by following signs north from Highway 48 in that village, while that in Peterborough is found by following signs from Highway 28.

"There's a boat over your head." The great lift locks at Peterborough and Kirkfield are the only pair of their kind in North America.

BOATS ON RAILS:
The Big Chute Marine Railway

The groaning lift locks at Peterborough and Kirkfield are not the only unusual structures on the Trent-Severn Waterway. About 40 kilometres north of Barrie, County Road 24 leaves the village of Coldwater and takes you 20 kilometres along a winding road, past farms and through forests to the Big Chute Marine Railway.

By the turn of the century, urbanites, fed up with the noise and fumes of the industrial cities, were finding a tranquil escape at places like the mouth of the Severn River. By 1906 there was increasing pressure to open up still more of the Severn, and the federal government gave approval to a marine railway that would guide the boats over the steep falls known as the Big Chute (a temporary railway already existed for workers then constructing a hydro generator station at the same location).

In 1920 the marine railway was finished, but by 1922 it needed enlarging. The new car was 4 metres wide by 11 metres long. It operated by being lowered into the water at one end, where the boats could be floated over the carriage and secured. The carriage was then winched out of the water and pulled along rails to the height of land where the cables were manually switched for the descent into the water at the other end.

Following the Second World War, recreational boating experienced an unprecedented boom. By the 1970s the outdated marine railway had become such a bottleneck that considerable enlargement was necessary. In 1977 a new carriage, 13 metres wide and 36 metres long, began to rumble up and down the granite cliff. Unlike the old car, the new carriage uses a modern system of four winches operated by digital control and automatic cable transfer. The older historic car is still used to handle overflow.

Viewing is easy. Parks Canada has created an attractive park with hiking and picnicking facilities. Amid the benches you may see concrete steps. These once led to the large houses that were home to the original workers in the hydroelectric plant. But it's the sight of a luxury yacht creaking up a cliff on a railway car that you won't easily forget.

The older of the cable cars at the Big Chute Marine Railway now handles overflow traffic.

48

The Petrolia Discovery theme park near the site of North America's first commercial well contains rigs and derricks that date back to the last century.

ONTARIO'S BLACK GOLD:
The Petrolia Discovery

So vast, modern and international has today's petroleum industry become that its modest roots have been forgotten. And those roots go back to a little town in southwestern Ontario aptly named Petrolia, where today a non-profit foundation, Petrolia Discovery, is striving to keep the legacy alive.

And it is succeeding. On the east end of Petrolia, the foundation operates a most unusual park. Here, on one of Canada's original oil fields, you can find oil rigs that date back a century. A central pumping plant known as a Fitzgerald Rig contains the biggest drive wheel ever built for a jerker rod system and has been operating off and on since 1903. From this building, wooden jerker rods slide back and forth across the oil field to operate pumps that urge oil from the ground. You can also see the gum beds that drew the first oil explorers to the area, and a cribbed well that shows how, at first, oil was dug rather than drilled.

Although Oil Springs, 12 kilometres south, represents the site of North America's first commercial oil well, dating from 1858, Petrolia contained the larger deposits. By 1866 the town had become a boom town of three thousand and a branch-line terminus for both the Grand Trunk Railway and the Canada Southern Railway.

Then, with the formation of the Imperial Oil Company in 1880, Petrolia became the centre of the British Empire's oil industry, a title it would retain for nearly twenty years. In that period, drillers and riggers travelled to all corners of the world, including today's war-torn countries like Iran and Iraq, to share the knowledge and skills that had quickly become legendary.

After the First World War, new refineries at Sarnia, along with the discovery of vast new reserves in Alberta, turned Petrolia into a near ghost town. But Petrolia Discovery has turned all that around. By bringing to the present a living snapshot of the oil industry's past, the park has revived the town. Local businesses have pumped money into streetscaping, while a costly restoration of the grand Victoria Hall has restored summer theatre to the town. A walking tour takes in the grand mansions of the oil barons, while a 4-kilometre fitness trail follows the ruins of the original oil fields.

At the site of the first well, the Oil Springs museum recounts that chapter in Ontario's oil history, although sadly, the village of Oil Springs has retained few oil heritage buildings. However, a short country drive takes you past privately owned fields where jerker rods still pull the crude from the ground as they have for a century and a half.

49

WEST MONTROSE:
The Last Covered Bridge

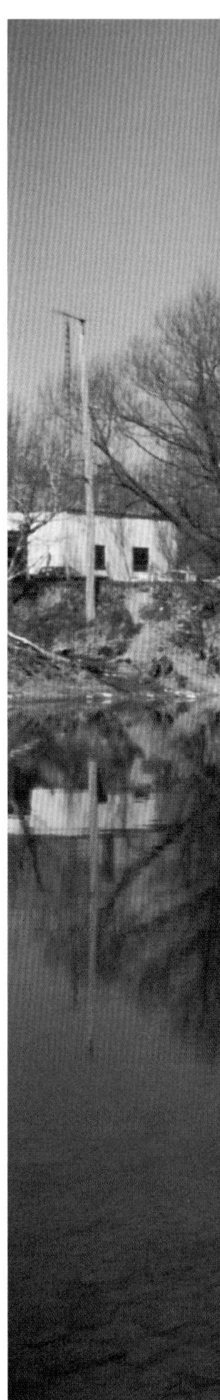

The clatter of hoofbeats and the groaning of a wagon wheel echo among the wooden rafters of the old covered bridge. A scene for a western movie? No, an everyday event at West Montrose, 15 kilometres north of Waterloo, just off Regional Road 22.

The area is heavily populated by the Old Order, "horse-and-buggy" Mennonites, and these black-garbed traditionalists frequently guide their horse-drawn wagons or buggies through what is Ontario's last covered bridge.

In an era when wood was less expensive and commonly used for bridge construction, walls and roofs were often added to prevent the deterioration caused by rain and heavy snow. Despite their utility and popularity in eastern Canada, Ontario's British army road builders steered clear of the technique, and fewer than a dozen were built in this province. The one at West Montrose is the only survivor.

Built in 1881 by a Mennonite barn builder named John Baer, it remained the Grand River's only crossing in the area until 1960, when a new concrete structure was completed less than a kilometre away. The bridge measures 60 metres long, and was illuminated by twenty shuttered windows and coal-oil lanterns, later replaced by electric lights. A feature rarely found on other covered bridges is the 1.8-metre overhang above each entrance.

To allow continued use of the historic structure, truss reinforcements have been added to the inside, the roof has been re-shingled and the substructure replaced. To complement this postcard scene, the village of West Montrose, huddled around the western approach to the bridge, has retained many of its simple nineteenth-century buildings. A part of pioneer Ontario can be both seen and heard at the West Montrose covered bridge.

Of Ontario's five historic covered bridges, the one at West Montrose on the Grand River is the only survivor.

PARIS PLAINS STONE CHURCH

Ontario's cities and countryside contain many magnificent stone buildings, from the huge blocks of red sandstone that form the Queens Park legislative buildings and the old city hall, both in Toronto, to the rubble stone that hardened pioneers gathered from the fields to make the handsome St. Margaret's Church on the Bruce Peninsula. But no stone construction technique is as distinctive or as delightful as the neat rows of cobblestones on the Paris Plains Church near the intersection of Brant County Roads 24A and 28, north of Paris, Ontario.

When Levi Boughton migrated from Rochester, New York, to Paris in the late 1840s, he brought with him a construction technique that few Upper Canadians had ever before seen. Originally devised by the ancient Romans during their occupation of England, it was a technique that could utilize common fieldstones, the bane of many farmers in the Paris and Brantford area, and create buildings of rare beauty.

The technique involved gathering thousands of field stones, usually dolomite or limestone, that had been relentlessly ground into spheres by the great glaciers and the swirling of their meltwaters. The stones would then be passed through a standard ring to ensure uniformity of shape and size. Then they would be laid in level "courses" to construct the walls of the buildings. The result was walls of incredibly uniform rows of cobblestones, almost as if they had been handmade.

The contractor for the church, and about a dozen other buildings in the town of Paris itself, was Philo Hull. Here, the technique was applied to a church, fences and several houses of different dimensions, making Paris the centre of this style. Later in the century, when brickmaking made construction so much cheaper, Boughton's cobblestone style died completely. Occasionally it is resurrected in individual homes, not because it is cheaper, but because of its rare beauty and grace. But back in Boughton's day it was an inventive way to turn a nuisance into a thing of beauty.

The unusual cobblestone walls on the Paris Plains Church near Brantford.

An unexpected site on Ontario's otherwise green landscape are these badlands near Cheltenham.

THE CHELTENHAM BADLANDS:
Ontario's Painted Desert

Many westward-bound Ontarians make Drumheller, Alberta, one of their must-sees. For here, thousands of years of water and wind erosion have worn through layers of shale to create a landscape of barren hills and gullies punctuated by remnant pillars known as "hoodoos." While the desert-like terrain spurned farmers and ranchers, it did expose coal seams and a rich source of dinosaur bones.

But drylands are expected in the west. They are less so in lush, forested Ontario. Known as Medina shale, a deposit of red-and-green sediment appears throughout the Niagara Escarpment area, but nowhere is it so dramatically exposed as in a 37-hectare hillside north of the village of Cheltenham. Here the shale has been sculpted into a dramatic landscape of smooth ridges and gullies, totally bereft of vegetation.

The age of the ancient seabed is estimated at 450 million years, not a period of dinosaur activity. And unlike those in Alberta, the feature here is not entirely natural. Until the settlers arrived, the deposit lay beneath a forest and soil cover. But once the settlers cleared the land and began to graze their cattle, erosion of the hillside exposed the colourful layers. So hard was the exposed material that grasses and shrubs were unable to take hold. However, like those in Alberta, Ontario's badlands revealed an economic resource, the ingredients for brickmaking, that brought a boom to the area.

The deposit also gave rise to a number of brickmaking villages in the area, such as Terra Cotta and the Cheltenham brickyards. When the brickmaking ceased, the villages dwindled. Terra Cotta remains a residential community, but the Cheltenham site now contains only the gaunt skeletal shells of the old kilns.

Located beside Old Baseline Road between Highway 10 and Mississauga Road, the ridges and gullies, with their colourful layers, have long been a local landmark, and destination for many a geography class. The dramatic landscape has also attracted film location scouts seeking unusual topography for their sets. The site was acquired by the Ontario government in 1999 and transferred to the Ontario Heritage Foundation. It is managed by the Bruce Trail Association as part of its trail system.

SLOMAN'S SCHOOL CAR:
The Schoolhouse that Rode the Rails

Many of us recall, some even fondly, the little red (or yellow) schoolhouses. For decades they dotted the Ontario countryside and were the educational mainstay of rural Ontario. Few of us, however, are aware that, through the wilds of northern Ontario, where only the railways linked little settlements isolated by miles of bush, the schoolhouses were in railway cars.

Between 1880 and 1914, five railway lines made their way through the forests of New Ontario, as the north was then called. At railside there grew a string of mill towns and hamlets for railway maintenance workers. But only a handful of divisional towns or industrial towns grew large enough to support their own schools.

By 1922, the population of these outposts was substantial, yet they had few facilities, no luxuries and no schools. A North Bay school superintendent named J. B. McDougall pleaded with the then Ontario premier, G. Howard Ferguson, to initiate a six-month experiment that would bring to the settlements a school on the back of a train.

Passenger cars were altered into classrooms containing desks, books, blackboards and a small apartment for the teacher. In 1926 the first two cars departed their display areas at the Canadian

The School on Wheels, Clinton, Ontario.

National Exhibition for northeastern Ontario. The experiment proved so successful that it was quickly made into a permanent program, and by 1938 seven such cars were operating across the northland.

For four days at a time the cars would rest at a siding in the tiny settlements, while children hiked or sledded for several kilometres for their precious education. Night school was provided for adults and the schoolcars became social gathering places for the area.

However, during the 1950s, the trackside settlements faded. The advent of diesel and a massive highway-building program turned them into ghost towns, and the schoolcars were no longer needed. One of the last, CNR No.15089, was shunted unceremoniously into a Toronto railyard in 1967.

After spending a few years with the Ontario Rail Association, car 15089 was put up for sale. A former student noticed the ad and eagerly phoned the family of the car's last teacher, Fred Sloman. (Fred Sloman was also the teacher who participated in the program the longest, from its inception in 1926 up to his retirement in 1965.)

To their credit, the people of Clinton, the home of Fred Sloman's widow, Cela, rallied behind the cause and brought the car to Clinton, where it was restored to its appearance as a schoolcar and opened as a museum. While many a country schoolhouse has received new life as a residence, the schoolhouse that rode on rails is one of a kind, and retells a story of northern life that would otherwise be forgotten.

53

Neglected and forgotten Niagara-on-the-Lake's Fort Mississauga now endures a barrage of golf balls from the course on which it sits.

FORT MISSISSAUGA:
The Forgotten Fort

Round and hard, the missiles speed through the air, crashing against the walls of the ancient fort. Bricks and mortar splatter into the air and fall to the ground.

Niagara-on-the-Lake's Fort Mississauga is being assaulted, not by enemy batteries, but rather by errant golfers on the golf course that now surrounds it. The fort was hurriedly built in 1814 on the site of an earlier Seneca fishing village from the rubble of an old lighthouse to stave off a repeat of an earlier American attack.

The fort sustained a garrison only until 1826. It was re-manned in 1837 during the Upper Canada rebellion of that year, and again during the American Civil War and the Fenian troubles. Later, it was used as a training camp during the various wars of the twentieth century. For all that, Fort Mississauga never had a hostile shot fired at it.

Although small, it remains the only example of a star-shaped military earthwork in Canada. In addition to the brick tower and the tunnel to the lake that you see today, the fort originally consisted of a barracks, guardroom and cells as well.

In 1976 when Parks Canada, which had so masterfully restored the much larger Fort George a short distance away, indicated its intention to restore Fort Mississauga, the golfers rebelled and won the day. Although Parks Canada has retained ownership and has stabilized the walls, they have left the fort a ruin. And that is what makes the fort unusual and enhances its appeal.

It is accessible along a trail from the corner of Front and Simcoe streets in the historic heart of the town. The town, of course, has much to offer the history lover, for it has retained its nineteenth-century ambience though careful preservation and restoration of many of its early buildings. The restored Fort George is worth a visit, as is the Niagara Apothecary, run by the Ontario College of Pharmacy as a Confederation-era drugstore. The town is best noted for its annual Shaw Festival, an event that brings theatre lovers to share the history of this picturesque Lake Ontario town.

THE CANAL THAT NEVER SAW WATER:
Newmarket's Ghost Canal

The wall of concrete looks enough like a canal lock, but 8 metres below your feet, where water and boats should be, you see grass and trees. You are standing beside the remains of a canal that never saw water, the Newmarket Canal.

The early decades of the nineteenth century were the canal era. At a time when railways were little more than science fiction and roads little better than quagmires, water was the only highway. The remarkable success of the Erie Canal in New York State sparked a spate of canal-building in Ontario. The Welland, the Rideau, and the Grand canals, parts of the St. Lawrence and Trent, had all made their appearance by the 1840s. And as early as 1800, Surveyor General Smith produced a map showing a canal linking Lake Ontario with Lake Simcoe along the Rouge and Holland river systems.

But by the time the smoke of steam engines ushered in the railway era around 1850, the Newmarket Canal still existed only on paper. With canals in decline, there seemed little point in proceeding. Then, in 1904, the Trent Canal was completed to Lake Simcoe, and politicians from the Newmarket area, led by their Liberal MP William Mulock, pushed once more for a link to that system. The engineers, however, cautioned that the watershed might not contain enough flow of water to properly operate the system. But with an election looming, the federal government went ahead anyway.

The canal was to be built in three sections. The first, from Lake Simcoe to Holland Landing, a distance of 15 kilometres, would be at lake level and require no lock structures. The second, from Holland Landing to Newmarket, a distance of 7 kilometres, would require three locks to cover the 14-metre rise in elevation. The third section would carry the canal to its completion at Aurora.

After the first two sections were finished, the First World War intervened, and in 1916 the canal project was cancelled. The engineers were proven right—there was too little water. One lock structure, minus gates, still stands in Holland Landing where old Yonge Street enters the village. Another, the best one to visit, lies about 3 kilometres east of Holland Landing. Here you can park your car in the conservation area and from the roadway see the old lock, surrounded by woods. You can also follow a trail that parallels the canal to Green Lane, where the remains of a swing bridge stand, now bypassed by the new four-lane roadway. A remnant of the third lock is visible in a park in the north end of Newmarket.

Although many Ontario canal projects either failed outright or declined economically, the Newmarket Canal remains as it began, high and dry.

This Holland Landing lock on the Newmarket Canal never saw water.

TEMPLE OF LIGHT:
The Sharon Temple

Much like modern-day cults, the religious denominations of early Ontario were occasionally fuelled by the quirks and charisma of dominant leaders. Groups like the Quakers and the Shakers, the Mormons and the Mennonites, all originated with "visionaries" who led a group of dedicated followers away from the mainstream denominations. While all were present in pioneer Ontario, none left so prominent a landmark as did David Willson and his Children of Peace.

In 1801, Willson, a Quaker, migrated from New York to the Newmarket area of Upper Canada, where his Society of Friends brethren (as the Quakers were called) were particularly active. However, Willson grew impatient with the local leadership and decided to have a vision of his own. His vision was to restore his form of Christianity to its Judaic roots.

In 1825, Willson and his Children of Peace began construction of an elaborate and highly symbolic temple. When finished, the three-storey structure resembled a windowed wedding cake and totally dominated the landscape of simple pioneer buildings. Centre doors on each side symbolized the equal acceptance of people from all directions, while the square shape, it is said, meant the group dealt "squarely" with everyone. Inside, twelve pillars represented the twelve apostles.

Then, as now, religious leaders displayed a strong sense of self. Inside the temple Willson placed a decorative altar that was partially enclosed, while on the grounds outside the temple he built his small but equally ornate personal study. The Children of Peace celebrated two festivals, Willson's own birthday, dubbed the "Feast of the Passover," and the fall "Feast of Illumination," when the Children placed 116 candles in their temple windows. Frequently described as a religious imposter, Willson was nonetheless acclaimed throughout Ontario for his lively travelling temple band.

Willson's death in 1866 signalled the downfall of the Children of Peace. By 1890 they were extinct, and the temple vacant. But in 1919, a far-sighted York Pioneer and Historical Society (ahead of even some modern groups) acquired the temple and converted it into a museum.

And so it remains today. On the outskirts of Sharon, now a Toronto suburb, visitors may view the temple, little changed in a century and a half. Although other pioneer buildings, including an 1852 township hall, have been moved onto the grounds, the story of David Willson and his Children of Peace brings to life a small but highly unusual chapter of our pioneer past. The site today is administered by the Sharon Temple Museum Society and stands at the corner of Leslie Street and Mount Albert Road.

One of the most unusual churches ever built in Ontario is Sharon Temple, built by the equally unusual Quaker sect known as the Children of Peace.

OPEN

THE DUTCH CHAPEL
The Pillars of the Scarborough Bluffs

Among southern Ontario's more unusual natural features are the Scarborough Bluffs. Not only do the craggy 20-kilometre-long forms loom up to 100 metres over Lake Ontario between the eastern end of the Beaches and the Rouge River, but their fractured and ever-eroding face reveals to scientists and laymen alike the mysteries of central Ontario's prehistoric past.

Unlike the tiny trickle that is today's Don River, Toronto was once the site of a mighty pre-glacial torrent, greater than the St. Lawrence. Here, more than seventy thousand years ago, these rushing waters poured into a great lake and there deposited an extensive delta. Then the ice age, with glaciers often more than 2 kilometres thick, deposited more boulder clay on top of the delta.

As the last ice sheets melted away twelve thousand years ago, and the lakes behind them drained, the delta stood like a mighty mesa above what was then a barren landscape. Wind, water and frost then began to eat away at its southern face. The alternating layers of soft, pure sand and rock-hard clay created oddly-shaped pinnacles and buttresses. So closely did the rugged shoreline resemble his beloved Yorkshire homeland, that Upper Canada's first governor, John Graves Simcoe, named them the Scarborough Bluffs.

In a quiet gully at the foot of Scarborough's Midland Avenue, erosion has created a series of buttresses somewhat like the architecture found in medieval European chapels, and geologists have named the area the Dutch Chapel.

The constant and unpredictable erosion has forced the removal of many homes, which had been built too close to the brink. At one time a local Scarborough Township councillor proposed that the cliff faces be covered with concrete to prevent further erosion, a fancy that was fortunately ignored.

Today, most visit "the Bluffs," as they are called locally, to picnic in the popular Bluffers Park located at the foot of Brimley Road. Here are beaches, restaurants, yachts, houseboats and unsightly marinas. But the centre of attraction remains the towering cliff face, within which is a story that is seventy thousand years old.

The Dutch Chapel, Scarborough Bluffs.

TORONTO ISLAND'S HAUNTED LIGHTHOUSE

Ontario's oldest standing lighthouse is haunted, some say, by the ghost of its first keeper. Constructed of huge limestone blocks, the hexagonal 20-metre structure was built in 1809 at Gibraltar Point, on what is now the Toronto Island archipelago, before there was a Toronto, and even before there were islands. (In 1834 the Town of York became the City of Toronto. The islands were actually a peninsula until 1858 when a vicious storm hurled waves across its narrow, sandy neck, severing it from the mainland.)

When the lighthouse was completed, John Paul Radan Muller was appointed its keeper and he moved into a small log cabin beside it. In April 1813, he watched helplessly as Colonel Pearce guided fourteen American ships past the lighthouse and landed the troops that would capture York, in one of the few American victories of the War of 1812.

Just two years later, Radan Muller disappeared in circumstances that the *York Gazette* described as "moral proof of having been murdered." It would later add that there was "no conviction of the supposed murder." Was he murdered by drunken companions? Did he renege on a bootlegging operation then being run from the military base? There was much speculation that bones later uncovered may have been those of the missing keeper.

Although the former whale-oil lamp has long since been replaced by more modern navigational aids, the lighthouse remains virtually unaltered. Yet, around it, an entire chapter in Toronto's history has started and finished. By the 1920s, the islands had become a popular recreational complex of amusement parks, hotels and private cottages. It was here in the island baseball stadium that baseball legend Babe Ruth hit his first professional home run into the waters of the lake.

Today, Gibraltar Point is a passive recreational area where trees, grass and trails have replaced the buildings of a bygone day. And the changes are all carefully watched over by the lighthouse and its keeper.

The old stone lighthouse on Toronto Island's Gibraltar Point is said to be haunted by its first keeper.

58

THOSE PERPLEXING PUKASKWA PITS

Some of Ontario's most unusual places predate recorded history. Early inhabitants left behind mounds, pits and paintings, features that filled crucial roles in their lives, but left question marks for a modern generation. While today's archaeologists may understand the paintings and the petroglyphs, no one has yet unravelled the mystery of the pukaskwa pits.

Found primarily around the shores of Lake Superior, pukaskwa pits (pronounced puk-a-saw) are manmade excavations dug into boulder beaches, which formed when the lake waters were about 30 metres higher than they are today. The conical pits are 2 or 3 metres across, with excavated stones piled protectively around the rim. Although clearly manmade, the lack of other evidence of human occupation, such as burial mounds, dumps or habitation areas, heightens their mystery. Archaeologists have found only bits of pottery, flints, and caribou bones, suggesting that the use of the pits was likely short-lived.

One theory suggests that they were vision pits. Young men of each tribe isolated themselves until the spirit of the animal that guided their lives visited them. Others speculate that the pits were shelters from the storm-tossed waters of the lake during the peak of the fur trade. Their location, close to the water but away from the waves, makes them excellent shelters for canoeists. Huddled inside, one is protected from the cold winds, while soaking up the sun. Some of the larger pits appear to have had hearths and possibly protective coverings.

The greatest concentration of pukaskwa pits is found along the northeastern shore of Lake Superior, where more than 250 are protected in Pukaskwa National Park. Because they can be easily altered, or even destroyed by accident or carelessness, their exact locations are not published. Pukaskwa Park epitomizes northern Ontario. Mountain peaks soar 640 metres high, wild rivers plunge through steep canyons, dense forests cloak the steep hillsides, and waves thunder against a rocky shore where cliffs loom high above the grey waters.

The park is accessed from Highway 17 by following Highway 627 through Heron Bay. Here you find the Friends of Pukaskwa store. From the campground and visitor centre, a 60-kilometre hiking trail leads along the coast to its end at Hattie Bay. A well-travelled canoe route follows the shore, with campsites at several locations. And although the locations of the mystery pits are not given, those who hike or canoe the shoreline of the park will quickly find a few of these mysterious holes and ponder their origin.

These unexplained excavations are found throughout Ontario.

This serpentine ridge is the legacy of a vanished culture that practised mound burials.

THE STRANGE SERPENT MOUND OF RICE LAKE

Ironically, the strongest visual evidence of Ontario's Native heritage deals not with life, but with death. Usually, places where Ontario's early peoples lived are seldom discernable to any but the trained archaeologist. Yet where they died can leave prominent physical features.

Take, for example, Rice Lake's unusual serpent mound. Although no other such mounds exist elsewhere in Canada, burial mounds in the shape of giant snakes are common in the Ohio Valley of the United States.

The mound on the north shore of Rice Lake is 2 metres high, 8 metres wide, and a twisting 60 metres long. Several other burial mounds, in the more common oval shapes, surround it. An example of the latter also exists at Tabor Hill Park in Scarborough, uncovered when the site was being prepared for housing. Archaeologists can't decide whether the serpent mound was intended to resemble a snake, since it lacks a "head," or was it an ordinary burial mound that was somehow extended.

Following the retreat of the glaciers around twelve thousand years ago, the Arctic-like area abounded in caribou, bison and possibly even mammoths. The first inhabitants were nomadic. As the climate warmed, forests covered the tundra, bringing smaller game like deer and rabbits. Berries and root crops became part of the staple diet. The time of the nomads was about to end.

Around 1000 BC, the mound-building culture entered the area. Originating in the Ohio Valley, it gradually made its way into Ontario, culminating in the collection of mounds on Rice Lake. No evidence suggests that this was a village site. The absence of bones from winter game indicates that it was, rather, a summer gathering place for trading, rice harvesting and burials.

Around AD 500 a revolutionary new way of life arrived. Corn and squash replaced hunting and gathering. Permanent villages were built, with longhouses surrounded by palisades. Pits, instead of mounds, were used for burials. The presence of burial pits just north of the mounds, and a habitation area west of them, confirms the existence of the new lifestyle. Consecutive harvests eventually leached the soil, and the inhabitants moved to more fertile grounds.

The arrival of the Europeans in the late eighteenth and early nineteenth centuries ended that way of life, as First Nations peoples were moved onto reserves. A logging dam near the outlet to Rice Lake flooded the rice beds, and a way of life ended forever. Today, the mounds are part of Serpent Mounds Park, where a long-vanished culture and custom can be interpreted by a modern world.

THE SOUTHWOLD EARTHWORKS:
A Pre-European-Contact Village Site

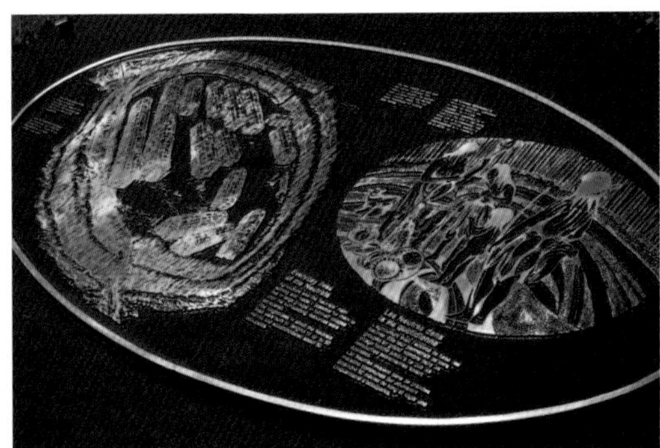

The flatlands of Elgin County stretch along the shores of Lake Erie, yielding some of Ontario's most fertile farmlands. Where the few forests remain, they contain Carolinian flora species. And farming has removed nearly all traces of early habitations. All except the unusual Southwold Earthworks.

Now a National Historic Site, these barely discernable lumps of earth represent a village site occupied by the Attiwonderonk prior to European contact, a Native group whose territory stretched from Chatham to Niagara Falls. Built about the time that Christopher Columbus was wandering around the Caribbean, the site consists of two circular mounds of earth separated by an apparent moat structure. The mounds represent the double row of palisades that surrounded the village, with gaps to indicate where a stream meandered through the site.

Research concludes that the outer mound is the older of the two. The palisades were built of tree trunks 4 to 5 metres high, driven into the ground and embanked with earth. The inner or later palisade consisted of two rows of trunks, indicating perhaps a concern for greater security. The double palisade is the site's most archaeologically significant component. Inside the compound were a number of the traditional longhouses, while fields of maize and squash surrounded the village.

By the time the first Europeans began ploughing the ground, likely during the Thomas Talbot settlements of the 1820s, the tribe had long vanished, possibly having fled the deadly Iroquois incursions of the 1640s. What is most astonishing about the site is that it survived the pioneer period, when homesteaders would not likely have recognized the site for what it was, nor cared. One wonders how many similar heritage treasures were lost to the plough during that time.

Despite its national heritage status, the site is barely developed. The only parking is along a widened shoulder on the road. Informational plaques indicate how the site was arranged, while a grassy pathway leads the quarter kilometre from the road into the stand of trees where the earthworks can be seen. The Southwold Earthworks are situated on County Road 14, about 3 kilometres south of Highway 3.

Once pallisaded, these prehistoric earthworks now appear as grassy mounds.

OJIBWAY:
The Case of the Missing Town

Across Ontario, towns were mapped out. Some remained small, some boomed, and some never made it off paper. But rarely were the sidewalks, hydrants, and roads built only to remain empty and unused.

Windsor, Ontario, grew in a most unusual way. While most towns started small, perhaps around a mill site or a port, Windsor was an amalgamation of planned company towns. The first settlement was known as Sandwich, and grew around a trading post on the Detroit River, later becoming the county seat.

But it was the infusion of large industrial company towns that gave the area its impetus to grow. Walkerville was laid out around Hiram Walker's whiskey distillery. Its neighbour, Ford City, was incorporated in 1913 as a residential community for that company's automotive plant.

Then there was Ojibway.

Ojibway differed from Walkerville and Ford City. While these predecessors used a traditional grid network of streets, Ojibway represented the latest in town planning. Streets radiated outward from three central squares, while a four-lane expressway linked it with Windsor, then 7 kilometres away.

Ojibway was to be an 1,800-acre company town for the American-Canadian Steel Corporation. Construction started during the First World War and continued into the 1920s. Objections, however, from Canadian steel producers, the effects of the Depression, and the presence of massive underground salt deposits beneath the proposed streets halted the project.

Although a few industrial buildings were completed, and the roads and sidewalks built, the population remained below one hundred. Over the rest of the townsite, grass and weeds claimed the streets and sidewalks, while forests took hold of the undeveloped area. By the 1960s, Ojibway had earned the distinction of being Canada's smallest organized municipality, with a population of a mere six.

Following Ojibway's inevitable annexation to Windsor in 1966, suburban growth spread onto the old townsite. New housing appeared on some of the original streets, and a racetrack was built in the middle of the "town." But much remained undeveloped. Grandly named streets like Broadview and Ojibway Parkway curved past open fields, where rusting hydrants poked above the tall grasses, while part of the planned four-lane express route became a local lane named Sandwich Street. But the strangest sight of all in this strangest of towns are the concrete sidewalks that cut straight through mature woodlots.

To reach the forest with the sidewalks, follow Normandy Street east from Malden. The doglegs in the first road following Ellis Street and Washington Boulevard represent the proposed streets, which now lead only through the woods. Concrete sidewalks line these dirt lanes, and at regular intervals cut straight into the forests.

Many of Ontario's communities have a strange history, but there are none so strange as Ojibway, the missing town.

This concrete sidewalk, once slated to serve homes, leads only through a silent woodlot.

Casa Loma's stable was as grand as the "castle" itself.

A HORSE PALACE:
The Casa Loma Stables

Casa Loma dominates Toronto's brochures, has felt the footsteps of millions of tourists, and has been the location of dozens of movie shoots. Toronto's best-known landmark is also its only castle. Less well known are the incredible Casa Loma stables. In fact, these elegant barns were finished a full four years before construction on the Casa even started. With their castle-like towers and turrets, they are considered the most lavish stables on the continent.

The castle's owner and builder was Sir Henry Pellatt. A multimillionaire, Pellatt earned his riches by investing in land along the newly built Canadian Pacific Railway to the west. He used those earnings to build Canada's first hydro generating station at Niagara Falls.

But he also loved the military and castles, and in 1905 he purchased twenty residential lots on top of the Davenport Escarpment. He then hired architect Edward James Lennox, designer of the city's most prominent buildings (including the old city hall), to design his castle. By 1914, the dream castle was complete on the outside. Huge cost overruns, however, prevented him from finishing the interior. After ten years, his wife's illness and financial ruin forced him to flee the castle.

Interestingly, the lesser-known stables more truly reflect the lifestyle and tastes of this mysterious man. Described as the most lavish anywhere on the continent, the buildings were completed in 1906. Inside, the stalls are of mahogany, with the horses' names spelled out in gold lettering above each. The floors were covered in Spanish tiles, laid in a herringbone pattern so that horses would not slip. Pellatt's favourite horse, named Prince, was even outfitted with a set of false teeth. Beneath the looming towers, the entrance is framed in white stone to contrast with the red brick of the building.

Adjoining the stables, the carriage house boasts a room larger even than the castle's main hall. Here, Pellatt stored his magnificent collection of carriages and Toronto's first electric car. The stables and carriage room are connected to the castle by a 150-metre-long tunnel.

Casa Loma and its stables are located on Spadina Road, north of Davenport.

THE YORKVILLE ROCK AND OTHER STRANGE PARKS

The rock is more than billion years old, weighs 650 tonnes and cost $300,000, yet it contains no precious metals or minerals. Plunked right in the middle of Toronto's priciest shopping district, it is known, somewhat derogatorily, as the "Yorkville Rock."

In 1966, Toronto's new east-west subway slashed through the hippy haven known as Yorkville Village, a collection of coffee houses tucked into a row of nineteenth-century homes. Although the little neighbourhood evolved into an ever-pricier shopping area, the subway route had left a no-man's land on which nothing heavy could be built. For years the strip of land remained an unsightly parking lot.

Finally, in 1991 the City of Toronto and the local business association hired architect Olesand Worland to create a park to befit both the context and the history of the area. In just one city block, his park would display the ecological variety of the entire province. While the trees and the flowers presented no problem, Toronto offered nothing that resembled Ontario's most extensive landscape element, the Canadian Shield, whose hard, rounded rocks are the oldest on earth. The nearest outcrops were over 150 kilometres away.

The solution he proposed was to move a granite outcrop from Gravenhurst to Toronto, a procedure that would cost more than a quarter of a million dollars. The first reaction was ridicule and outrage; however, the park not only proceeded, but opened in 1994 to widespread acclaim from architects and users alike. In one city block the visitor can travel from a garden with bluebells and trilliums to an alder grove, a wetland, and a herb garden. At the end of the provincial mini-tour, the visitor has lunch or reads a book on top of a billion-year-old rock. The park stretches along the south side of Cumberland Avenue, between Avenue Road and Belair.

Although equally acclaimed, the award-winning Cloud Garden, in the heart of Toronto's financial district, has fared less well. In contrast to the much-visited Yorkville park, Cloud Garden is little more than a haven for the homeless and a gathering place for downtown bike couriers.

Designed by Margaret Priest, the small lot on Temperance Street between Yonge and Bay contains urban woodland, waterfalls, and an observation platform. Situated over the entrance to a parking garage is a glass enclosed "Cloud Forest" conservatory, with its recreation of a tropical rain forest. Surrounded by the glass towers of the Bay Street brokers, this intriguing urban park won a Governor-General's Medal for Architecture in 1994 and a merit award from the Canadian Society of Landscape Architects the next year.

The Yorkville rock sparked controversy when it was moved from Gravenhurst to Toronto.

No discussion of Toronto's unusual green spaces is complete without the Sculpture Garden. Located on the south side of King Street East, opposite the imposing St. James Cathedral, this outdoor gallery gives sculptors free rein to display their creations and has hosted seventy artists in more than fifty exhibits. Created in 1981 with donations from Louis Odette, it is administered by a voluntary advisory board. You never know what you will come across at this one!

The Don Valley Parkway's elevated wetlands.

PERFECT PURIFICATION:
The Elevated Wetlands of the Don Valley

The elevated wetlands of the Don Valley have drivers on the busy Don Valley Parkway blinking in disbelief. At the Don Mills Road exit are a half dozen massive plant pots. To some, they may look more like giant topless teapots, to others, grotesque mastodons performing some form of daisy chain. They are in fact an innovative system of purifying the waters of the Don River using only plastic.

In 1995, the Canadian Plastics Industry Association hired artist Noel Harding to create a public work of art that would help illustrate the artistic potential of that industrial material. Harding, a sculptor who pushes the limits of both sculpture and material, is well known for his Potato Eaters sculpture. This series of metal structures is 12 to 25 metres high, each containing a living tree, and helped earn him international attention at the Atlanta Olympics.

Inside the giant pots in the Don Valley are various types of plastic, all shredded, including bottles, resins, auto fluff and geo textiles. A cluster of solar panels pumps water from the Don River into the highest of the pots. Here, plants, shrubs and trees draw the pollutants and toxins from the water and return it perfectly pure. More than seventy different industries helped sponsor the unusual project, including fifty plastics industries. The sculptures, which measure between 8 and 15 metres high, were created between 1997 and 1998 and developed from a prototype developed at the University of Lethbridge.

Harding's is not the only effort underway to clean up the river. A short distance downstream, the Friends of the Don won a $100,000 grant from the Ontario government to excavate a century and a half of industrial residue from the flood plain. They replaced the landfill with a natural wetland ecosystem which, like the elevated wetlands, provides free water purification.

The strange sculptures can be seen up close from Taylor Creek Park on Don Mills Road, just north of the Don Valley Parkway. The new marshland lies to the south of the Bloor Viaduct and can be accessed from the bike trail that follows the valley.

LAST OF A KIND:
Blair's Sheave Tower

The wooden tower stands in the middle of the woods near the historic community of Blair, looking like a miniature mining headframe. But this tapering wooden structure, which rises four storeys above a rushing stream, is a rare relic of pioneer Ontario — a sheave tower.

Sheave towers were accessories to grist mills. They used the force of the river to turn a sheave, or grooved wheel, and were connected by a pulley to a water-powered grist mill. A local mill owner named Allan Bowman built the tower at Blair in 1876 to power the nearby Carlisle grist mill. The original mill, a five-storey structure built in 1849, burned in 1928. Following the fire, the power from the sheave tower produced electricity until 1954.

Long a favourite of local artists, photographers and historians, it was partially restored in 1962 by the Waterloo Historical Society. Runoff from nearby housing developments, however, rushed into the creek, where it damaged the foundation and put the building's future at risk.

Blair, however, is one of those heritage-conscious communities. So while the owners of the tower worked to clear the sluiceway of silt, the local council voted, in 1986, to declare it a heritage structure, to help reduce the threat of demolition. In 1994 it was bought, in turn, by the Cambridge chapter of the Architectural Conservancy of Ontario.

Four years later renowned heritage architect Nicholas Hill was hired to restore the crumbling ruin. Hill had been responsible for more than a dozen community heritage plans, as well as restoration of the Kingsville, Ontario, railway station and the University of Guelph's Cruickston Park mansion and grounds.

Because much of the tower's wood had rotted, many original planks required replacing (although for some preservationists preservation versus replication presents a dilemma). But in 2000, the restored tower was unveiled to commemorate the village's two hundredth anniversary. Sadly, Hill died the following year, at just fifty-eight.

The heritage of Blair goes beyond the sheave tower. The village began life as a milling centre on Blair Creek, close to the Grand River, where today, the urban sprawl from Cambridge creeps ever closer. Yet the historic integrity of Blair continues to survive, as hotels, homes, mills and cemeteries that date from the early days of settlement have been retained. But of all the saved and restored historic buildings, the sheave tower, the only one of its kind left in Ontario, remains the most unusual.

Blair's strange sheave tower resembles a miniture mining headframe.

66

KITCHENER'S PIONEER TOWER:
Cultural Cooperation

The Kitchener area of Ontario, noted for farmers' markets, Mennonite cuisine, and a rousing Oktoberfest, is also Ontario's unlikely capital of unusual towers. Besides the rustic sheave tower near Blair, Kitchener has the stone pioneer tower.

Dominating the Grand River Valley from one of its loftiest banks, the tower was built to commemorate Ontario's first inland pioneers. French settlements had existed along the Detroit River near Windsor as early as the 1760s. The United Empire Loyalists followed in the 1780s along the shores of Lake Ontario and Lake Erie. With the arrival of Joseph Schoerg and Samuel Betzner in 1800 came the vanguard of Ontario's inland pioneers.

By 1805, the German Company had purchased over 60,000 acres of land along the Grand River from the Mohawks, who had received it as a reward for their service to the British during the American Revolution. Soon, columns of Conestoga wagons were lumbering northward carrying Pennsylvania Dutch and Mennonite settlers. These savvy farmers, with their commitment to farming as a divinely ordained way of life, established one of Ontario's most prolific agricultural communities.

The idea for the tower came more than a century later. To help heal the nationalist wounds caused by the First World War, and to celebrate the German origins of the Waterloo area, William Breithaupt promoted the idea of a pioneer memorial tower.

Designed by Toronto architect W. A. Langton, the tower was officially opened August 28, 1926, and was immediately declared a National Historic Site by the Historic Sites and Monuments Board. The 22-metre-high tower is topped with a copper spire of Swiss influence and a weather vane that commemorates the arrival of the colonists in their Conestoga wagons. The body of the tower, made of reinforced concrete, is faced with fieldstones to reflect the hardships in clearing the fields. Visitors enter through a doorway of Indiana limestone and climb to an eight-sided observation deck. Four glazed windows light the stairs. From the deck the view incorporates long stretches of the historic waterway.

In 1939, concerned over declining maintenance, the Historic Sites Branch took over the tower and upgraded the grounds, planting grass and adding a parking area.

Farm buildings of the pioneering Betzner and Schoerg families still stand nearby. In the 0.5-hectare park beside the tower, their family graves are the oldest non-Aboriginal inland burial grounds in Ontario. The tower is not staffed and has no admission charge. It lies at the end of Pioneer Tower Road, which you can reach by following Deer Ridge Drive east from Kitchener's King Street. The site is part of the Woodside National Historic Site in Kitchener.

This stone tower commemorates the heritage of the German pioneers in the Waterloo County area.

EMO'S UNUSUAL NORLUND CHAPEL

Many churches have lost their steeples, sometimes to fire, sometimes to old age. But the Norlund Chapel in Emo, Ontario, is a steeple that has lost its church.

Emo is located in the far northwestern reaches of Ontario. Here, the surprising land is flat and the soil is black and almost treeless. Geologically, this part of Ontario is an extension of the prairie landscape. To reach this rich land, the first settlers travelled along the wide Rainy River by steamer. Along the way villages grew up around the many little steamer landings. In 1904, the railway arrived, eliminating the role of many of the steamer villages.

Midway between the railway towns of Fort Frances and Rainy River, Emo got a station and became a busy town. But its origins as a steamer stop remain visible, with a main street that developed along the riverfront. As it grew, Emo attracted businesses, schools and churches. In 1935, St. Patrick's Roman Catholic Church was built on the outskirts of the village. Its 12-metre-high wooden steeple was topped with a 2-metre-high wrought-iron cross fashioned by a local blacksmith.

In 1971, lightning struck and destroyed the church. Incredibly, the steeple survived, nearly unscathed. To celebrate the miracle, Elmer Norlund and Ed Sletmoen designed a chapel around the steeple. Its diminutive size, just 2 metres by 3, is barely enough to allow eight people to fill the building. Now nondenominational, it is open to worshippers of all faiths. The Emo steeple is one of the world's smallest churches, and can be found on the north side of Highway 11/71 at the village limits.

Norlund Church in Emo—a steeple without a church.

THE CRYPTIC GRAVESTONE OF RUSHES CEMETERY

Visitors to the Rushes pioneer cemetery, west of Kitchener, have long scratched their heads in puzzlement at the mass of letters that cover the strange grave marker. While the size of the stone and the graphic etched on it are not unlike those found on thousands of other nineteenth-century grave markers, the message definitely is not. For covering the entire face of the gravestone is a mass of 225 letters and numbers with no apparent order or sense. Yet the message is in there, if you can figure it out.

Rushes Cemetery is an ordinary-looking pioneer cemetery. Situated atop a hill, the cemetery is neatly trimmed and surrounded by rolling farmland. Cars rush past on the busy road, while an occasional Mennonite buggy creaks by at a more leisurely pace. But it is in the far corner of Rushes cemetery that the now famous "Bean marker," with its cryptic inscription, attracts the most attention.

Samuel Bean was born in 1842 in Wilmot Township, and became an Evangelist minister as well as a medical doctor. Local legend claims he also read the entire Bible sixty-five times. In 1865 he married Henrietta Furry, who died only seven months later. His second marriage, to Susanna Clegg, didn't last much longer. To commemorate their passing, Bean devised what may be one of Ontario's most mystifying and most-visited grave markers, with what at first glance is a nonsensical and random arrangement of letters that totally cover the front of the marker.

While the dedication may appear impossible to decipher, by determining where to start the message and the order in which the words are spelled, the message is suddenly and plainly revealed. The original grave marker had deteriorated to the point where the letters became unreadable. But to help keep alive this interesting piece of local lore, heritage proponents in 1982 erected a duplicate stone beside the original.

Happily, Bean's third marriage lasted longer and he now lies buried by his third wife in the cemetery in Strasbourg, Ontario.

The grave marker itself is illustrated here, and the reader is invited to try and solve the puzzle. Clue: don't start at either the top or the bottom. Rather, begin at the seventh column from the left, and at the seventh letter from the top. The answer is at the back of this book.

Rushes cemetery is located 3 kilometres north of the attractive country village of Wellesley, on Waterloo Regional Road 5.

Can you solve the message on this odd grave marker?

See page 206 for the answer.

GONE HOME
BEAN
HENRIETTA
SUSANNA
S V W E T B S A 15 S T M O R E
E I R T E 2 Y D & H N S 10 H E
M I A D 17 & S H T N O A R M T
N A Y D H D. N E F S M Y E H E
E N S O W M. A B E O 2 D 26 T T
E V & E I R O M I F S G E E E
H R S 27 D I I E T W R 7 A O M
D A U H T A N M I S A 8 6 B. T
H T S E S M E R E T E L I E S.
Y E A I P H N I T A Y R I P M
E W N 8 6 5 A G E D 23 A P E L
E R N H S N W F W O I D T D H
I G A I 2 D I E H D E 27 H G O
T F R M O B T R N W N E V N A
F S O G D U A E O I H A E M Y
READER MEET US IN HEAVEN

This Northern Ontario monument recalls a tragic labour dispute.

MONUMENT TO MURDER:
Massacre at Reesor Siding

Unlike the more popular Trans-Canada Highway, which follows the spectacular shore of Lake Superior, there is another "trans-Canada highway." Numbered as Highway 11, it passes through northeastern Ontario, offering landscapes that are much less dramatic. Much of it traverses the northern Clay Belt, where sleepy railway towns appear at regular intervals throughout the flat farmlands. It comes as a surprise then to see above an overgrown field a monument to a murder.

After the First World War, plans to colonize the area failed when the ex-soldiers and city dwellers recoiled at the harsh conditions and returned south. During this flight, many of the railway towns failed too. Reesor Siding was one of them. The only industry there was supplying logs to the Spruce Falls pulp mill in Kapuskasing, or working in the bush camps.

In January of 1963, more than one thousand members of the Lumber and Sawmill Workers Union working in eight bush camps staged a wildcat strike to protest the slow progress of contract talks. But they weren't the only suppliers of logs. Local farmers also hauled logs from their own lots as independent contractors, and they had no affiliation with the union. Suspicious of unions, they refused to support the strike and continued to pile their logs at nearby Reesor Siding for shipment to the mill.

Tensions ran high. The company refused to negotiate until the workers returned to the camps. The workers refused to return until the company began to negotiate. Calls for the provincial government to appoint a conciliator went unheeded. The government then made the situation worse by granting permits to the independent farmers to continue to supply logs. Frustrated by the lack of progress, and angered by the farmers' antipathy, the strikers began to vandalize the log piles at the siding

On the night of February 11, four hundred strikers marched on the siding to once again unpile the logs. Alerted by the police, the farmers, now armed, huddled in a cabin waiting for them. Shots rang out in the cold night air and three strikers fell dead. Another eight lay wounded.

Twenty of the farmers were brought to trial, charged with "non-capital" murder. Without proof of who fired the guns, they were acquitted. Meanwhile, more than two hundred strikers were convicted of participating in a riot and fined. To commemorate the tragic deaths of the union strikers, the United Brotherhood of Carpenters and Joiners has erected a large monument, which rises incongruously above the flat landscape of the deserted siding and speaks for itself. In a fitting act of irony, the workers now own the mill.

THE SUDDEN SPLENDOUR OF THE ELORA GORGE

Suddenly and unexpectedly, in the flat farmlands northwest of Guelph, there appears a crack. No ordinary crack, the Elora Gorge is a canyon 2 kilometres long and more than 20 metres deep— a wonderland of hanging gardens, caves, caverns, dry valleys and odd-looking rock formations.

The gorge represents the outcropping of a dolostone formation known by geologists as the Guelph Formation, rich in fossils and reefs, and four hundred million years old. When the glaciers left the area about twenty thousand years ago, the waters began to wear down the rock until a long gorge took shape. The remnant of that post-glacial torrent is today's Grand River.

The various shapes and formations found in the gorge have fanciful names. Dividing the river into a foaming waterfall, the Tooth of Time is formed by the remains of an eroded ledge. Close by, the Lovers' Leap promontory juts into the fork formed by Irwin Creek and the Grand River. Frther downstream, castles were etched by the waters of a long-vanished river that plunged over the edge of the cliff, leaving a series of rock columns that resemble castle ramparts. An extinct waterfall has carved out a 40-metre-wide amphitheatre known as the Punch Bowl.

The Cascade is the filmy plunge of a small creek into the gully. Across from it the Hanging Garden shows off various mosses and ferns drooping from an overhanging cliff. Several caves along the riverbank make unusual swimming holes, and the Hole in the Wall provides passage for a trail right through the rock itself.

But hidden under the nearby farmlands there also lies an earlier pre-glacial gorge, which parallels today's defile. While the existence of this mystery gorge is revealed only through the drilling of local wells, it can be seen near Fergus where the route of the earlier gorge crosses that of the newer one, causing the rocky wall of today's gorge to vanish at that point.

The strange beauty and the appeal of the rushing river have turned the gorge into a popular park. Trails follow both riverbanks and wind along the bottom of the gorge. Inner tubes are rented to those who wish to cool off on a hot summer day by floating downstream and viewing the gorge in its entirety and without obstruction.

The Elora Gorge Conservation Area, which also has campgrounds, is a short distance southwest of the popular village of Elora.

This unexpected crack in flat farmland contains many unusual rock formations.

Fossil hunters can dig the ancient critters right out of the mud.

FOSSIL HUNTERS' FANTASY:
The Rock Glen Gorge

While no one is going to find any dinosaur bones in the Rock Glen Gorge, they will find hundreds of equally ancient creatures. Located in the Rock Glen Conservation Area, the gorge was created by the relentless erosion of the Ausable River into layers of limestone and shale. As the ancestors of today's shellfish died they drifted to the bottom of an early ocean, where they hardened into rock. Above them, more layers were deposited, and they also hardened. When the last glaciers finally melted, the water of today's Ausable River eroded into the soil and then into bedrock to gradually expose the former seabeds and their trove of early critters.

Fossils appear in much of Ontario's bedrock, and most usually require a pick to remove. But what makes the fossils in the damp little gully so unusual is that during rainfalls the shale turns soft enough to allow the shells to be removed by hand. The most common fossils found here are the branch-like staghorn coral or plant-like crinoids. Less common are the snail-like trilobites. The most interesting are the butterfly-shaped brachiopods, which the Chinese call "stone butterflies." While the fossils can be found throughout the little valley, the footing is tricky. The hunting grounds lie deep in the 25-metre chasm, where the stream trickles around boulders.

Rock Glen Conservation Authority has a few rules. Picks and shovels are not permitted, nor is collecting from the valley walls themselves. Loose sediments, however, are everywhere, and here you can help yourself. The park has a museum and staff with helpful brochures. The 25-hectare conservation area is on Lambton County Road 12, close to the village of Arkona, in southwestern Ontario.

ALGONQUIN PARK'S INCREDIBLE BARRON CANYON

At first glance it is hard to believe that Ontario has a canyon so deep and so precipitous. While the magnificent Ouimet Canyon in northern Ontario is longer and wider and displays a collection of rare Arctic plants, the canyon on the Barron River in northeastern Algonquin Park is both narrower and considerably deeper.

Its origins are as unique as the canyon itself. After the rocks of the Canadian Shield were formed billions of years ago, they lay buried beneath the deposits of an ancient sea. Under the waters of that sea, the sandy deposits gradually hardened into limestone. When the entire area heaved upward, the limestone cap fragmented into fault lines that ran in a northwest to southeast direction.

Millions of centuries later, as the great ice sheets that covered Ontario retreated northward, the meltwaters drained along the fault lines. One channel became the outlet for an enormous post-glacial lake named Lake Algonquin. Some geologists estimate that the torrent equalled a thousand Niagaras, one of which gradually carved out the Barron Canyon. As the ice sheet continued its northerly retreat the meltwaters found a lower outlet that became the Mattawa and Ottawa Rivers.

Since then, erosion has continued its sculpting magic on the canyon. The harsh freeze-and-thaw action of the frigid Algonquin winters cause chunks of rock to fragment and cascade into the valley far below.

For a few decades the Barron River echoed to the shouts of loggers pushing their logs downstream to mills at Petawawa and Pembroke. After the last drive ended in 1936, the cleft became an awe-inspiring destination for canoists and hikers. Birdwatchers observed such unlikely species as the swamp-loving yellow-bellied flycatcher and the common yellowthroat along the cliffs, as well as rare bald eagles.

Thanks to Algonquin's park planners the canyon is easy to visit and photograph. From the parking area 11 kilometres west of the Sand Lake gate, a 1.5-kilometre loop trail leads to the lip of the precipice, a dizzying 100 metres above the river below. The trail is occasionally steep and the edge unfenced. From the top, breathtaking views extend far downstream to the east. Canoes can launch at a number of landings. The portion of the river between the soaring walls is relatively placid, with only a few portages, and makes for a pleasant afternoon to view one of Ontario's more unusual and spectacular geological wonders.

The dizzying Barron River canyon is the most spectacular chasm in Ontario.

THE HELL HOLES OF EASTERN ONTARIO

A walk through the forest can sometimes be a dangerous thing, not necessarily from wolves or bears or even deer hunters, but from a careless step into a hole, especially when the hole leads to Hell.

The limestone ridge along the Salmon River north of Napanee contains some of the area's most unusual natural features. There are caves, crevices, and odd-looking rock columns. But the strangest of the oddities are what locals call the "Hell Holes."

To early settlers unfamiliar with geology, these holes in the forest floor seemed to have no end. While most are little larger than foxholes, a few are large enough to allow a human to squeeze through. Those who braved the descent found caverns that stretched in many directions.

Geologists refer to these phenomena as "karst" features. Karst topography occurs when soft limestone layers beneath a hard upper layer dissolve in water. This weathering causes caves and caverns, and the Hell Holes. Similar to caves, the holes in the forest floor can open into large, pitch-black rooms, one of which was once large enough to hold twenty people (it later collapsed). While there are other locations in Ontario with similar features, the ridge by the Salmon River, near the village of Roblindale, offers the greatest concentration of these cavities.

Most are located in the privately run Hell Holes Park. Here, a self-guided trail, a little over 3 kilometres long, leads not only to the strange holes, but over natural rock bridges, through eerie canyons lined with layered cliffs and columns, and then to the Devil's Horses' Stable hole, 7.5 metres deep and 2.5 by 3.5 metres square. A ladder leads to those depths.

Hell Holes Park is located on Centreville Road about 5.5 kilometres east of Highway 41, and 10.7 kilometres north of Highway 401 (Exit 579). Snacks, gifts and, of course, flashlights are available in the log cabin shop. It is said that one visitor even took his wedding vows in the Hell Holes. The duration of this marriage is not known.

Early pioneers thought that these bottomless pits led straight to Hell.

Crawford Lake is one of only two deep oxygen-deprived meromictic lakes in Ontario.

THE LAKE WITH NO WAVES:
The Strange Story of Crawford Lake

The Crawford Lake Conservation Area is a rare find. It sits atop the Niagara Escarpment with wonderful views and trails that wind through a hardwood forest. It also has a small lake, but this is a lake with no waves.

Geologists even have a special name for it, a meromectic lake, which means that, relative to its surface area, it is disproportionately deeper than most lakes, to the point that waves seldom occur and the bottom sediments remain undisturbed. In effect, it is ecologically like two lakes, one on top of the other. The lower levels are deprived of the oxygen that would normally come from the air above, thus preserving the material on the bottom.

Such preservation allows scientists to read this debris and determine with much more certainty what the area around it was like thousands of years ago. Lake Crawford is estimated to be at least fifteen thousand years old.

Among the layers of silt that cover the bottom, scientists uncovered evidence of early Huron habitation. This discovery sent archaeologists searching the area around the lake, where they uncovered the remains of a previously unknown Huron village. The village contained nine longhouses and a population of about 450, and dates from around AD 1430. Numerous other village sites were subsequently recorded in the surrounding hills and valleys.

Not only is the shape and morphology of the lake unusual, so too is its origin. Unlike other lakes, which form along existing rivers or in lowlands, this one occurred, some theorize, when a cave beneath the upper limestone layer suddenly collapsed. Water rushed in from underground streams, quickly filling the cavity. Another theory suggests that the lake fills an ancient post-glacial spillway.

In 1969 the land was sold to the Halton Region Conservation Authority, which laid out trails and recreated the Huron village, complete with palisade. So authentic is the habitation and the depiction of the lifestyles of its inhabitants that it has become a must-see for many school children from across Ontario

A 1.4-kilometre path leads to the lake from the gate, where interpretive signs explain its unusual origins and composition. A 7.2-kilometre trail leads further afield, through the dark woodlands, to a lookout point over the scenic Nassagaweya Canyon. The park is on the Guelph Line, a short distance south of Highway 401.

75

ONTARIO'S SOUTHERN PRAIRIE

Most believe that Ontario first consisted of dense, dark forests broken only by small Native clearings. But prairies? Not only were they widespread, but one of the largest remnants is right inside the city of Windsor.

Before European settlers marched across Ontario, axe in hand, Ontario's forests were interspersed with more than 750 square kilometres of tall-grass prairie and oak savannah. Of this total, nearly two thirds was located within today's Essex, Kent and Lambton Counties. Smaller prairie landscapes occurred in Elgin County, near Rice Lake, Lake Simcoe and even within today's Greater Toronto Area.

Typically, the tall-grass prairies consisted of blue stem grass up to 3 metres high, prairie cord grass and Indian grass, while here and there in the meadows stood oak trees. Such open areas were irresistible to settlers, and the treeless soils were quickly put to the plough.

An accident of history, however, spared a remnant of tall-grass prairie near Windsor. Prior to the arrival of the British, the French had settled much of the Windsor area. Because the Detroit River was their first means of transportation, they congregated close together along the river front, their farms divided into long, thin strips of property. Because the rear portions were so far from the river, the prairie on them was left unattended and remained largely unaltered. Though industrial and residential development was proposed for the area, wars and depressions intervened, and by the 1950s these prairie backlands remained in a largely natural state.

In 1971, recognizing that this landscape represented the last 1 percent of Ontario's ancient prairies, the Department of Lands and Forests, the Quetico Foundation and the Nature Conservancy of Ontario purchased the properties, to manage and preserve this nearly vanished natural legacy. Now safely within the Ojibway Prairie Provincial Nature Reserve, this 105-hectare remnant is managed carefully. Because one the natural forces in the creation of prairies is fire, management practices include controlled burns in the spring. Flowering plants and the tall grasses are in full bloom by August.

Besides the reserve, the City of Windsor manages a larger area known as the Ojibway Prairie Complex, a 137-hectare series of four parks, which includes interpretation centres and trails. Access to the provincial reserve and the other parks is via Matchette Road in the west end of Windsor.

Tall grasses dominated one of Ontario's unusual prairie landscapes.

THE BIG SAND PILE:
Houghton's Sand Hill

Towering more than 120 metres above the waters of Lake Erie, Ontario's biggest sandbox, the Houghton Sand Hill, stands higher than even the Scarborough Bluffs. As the glaciers of the last great ice age melted northward, a huge lake, four times the size of Lake Erie, formed along the edge of the ice lobe. As the torrents of meltwater raced into the lake, a huge delta took shape. The glaciers melted back still further, allowing the great lake to drain away, leaving today's Lake Erie and a monster pile of sand. The winds began to blow across the treeless wasteland, and the sand piled into huge dunes that towered above the lake.

Thousands of years later, as settlers took up land in the nearby forests, this geological phenomenon did not go unnoticed. In 1877, the *Atlas of Norfolk County*, normally a conservative and understated tome, gushed uncharacteristically that there was "nothing more astonishing than the immense mounds of pure sand, standing upon the edge of the precipitous cliffs which border the lake."

One of the first to take advantage of the heights was the United States Lake Survey, which placed an 18-metre observatory on the summit. A similar tower on Long Point, and a third across the lake in Pennsylvania helped map the navigation charts used by sailors to this day.

The sand hill attracted curiosity seekers as well. In the 1890s, George Alton, the owner, charged ten cents a visit. A geological oddity was quickly becoming a tourist attraction. But the hill came perilously close to extinction when a glass manufacturer tried to purchase the sand for export to the United States. Alton resisted, and the sand pile was saved.

Then in 1958 a campground was opened. Constant improvement to the unusual grounds have made it one of the more popular privately owned attractions on Lake Erie. From the roadside, the hill looks like an uninspiring grassy mound. A short walk to the top reveals the dizzying height above the lake below. Pure sand from crest to beach, the bluffs display ever-changing layers and shapes. For the kids, the hill is a huge sandbox, where they can tumble down the gentler slopes, or build endless castles.

Sand Hill Park is located 12 kilometres east of Port Burwell on Regional Road 42.

Ontario's biggest "sandbox" towers 120 metres above Lake Erie.

THE TORRANCE BARRENS:
Scary

In the middle of the idyllic Muskoka Lakes country, known throughout North America for its classical Canadian beauty, lies an oddly barren and desolate landscape. So eerie and unusual is this landscape that Canadian film director David Cronenberg, master of the horror movie, chose the area as the location for his bizarre film *Naked Lunch*.

The Muskoka Lakes, one of Canada's premier recreational playgrounds, lie in the ancient granite heart of the Canadian Shield. Sparkling lakes nestled amid the pine-laden outcrops inspire artists and photographers. Thus, the desolation found in the Torrance Barrens seems dramatically out of place.

The barrens are located south of the village of Torrance, and cover nearly 2,000 hectares. On this vast outcropping of bare and windswept rock, vegetation is rare. Here and there, where oak seeds have found a rare patch of shallow soil, stubby shrubs struggle to grow. Between the low rock ridges are ponds and areas of dank swamp. The clean, smooth rock surfaces are a result of glacial scouring and constant washing of the waves in the large lakes, which followed the retreating ice lobes.

Today, this rare ecosystem is a conservation reserve with a system of short trails that lead from a small parking area. In 1999, the Barrens were further designated as a "Dark Sky Reserve." With the near absence of habitation and the unobstructed view from horizon to horizon, the conditions are ideal for amateur astronomers and stargazers. Using the designation, the municipality is able to control the type of night lighting within a buffer of 5 to 8 kilometres around the reserve.

The barrens lie along the Southwood Road, Regional Road 13, and begin just south of Highway 169 at Torrance.

David Cronenberg filmed a movie at the eerie Torrance Barrens.

A CITY FOR THE BIRDS:
Picton's Birdhouse City

In the shadow of a cliff near Picton, Ontario, there lies a city that is strictly for the birds. Started in 1978 by the Prince Edward Region Conservation Authority, Birdhouse City is a collection of more than eighty birdhouses. Not just any birdhouses, they have been designed to copy many of the area's actual buildings. The city is the legacy of former authority superintendent Doug Harnes, whose skill in woodworking led to the creation of this bird city's first structures.

The first to be built was a recreation of the Massasauga Park Hotel. Measuring more than 1.5 metres square, it was supported by two poles and boasted three thousand miniature shingles. Pretty soon everyone got into the act, and birdhouses of all descriptions began to show up. Participants in Experience '80 contributed a paddle wheeler, a police car and a "fly-in" theatre, while the local McDonald's donated, naturally, a McDonald's "fly-through."

Visitors arrive, often by the busload, to see a Greek temple, a Pennsylvania Dutch barn, and Picton's historic Crystal Palace, while the "departed" can find comfort in the "Nest In Peace" Funeral Home.

Nor was city planning overlooked. The architectural drafting class of Prince Edward Collegiate planned the city with streets like Finch Avenue and Swallow Drive. The Lake Ontario Cement Company donated labour and material for a central fountain.

Sadly, due to financial constraints, many of the structures have seen maintenance slip, and several need repair and repainting. Still, birds love it. The purple martins, the wrens and the bluebirds flit from cottage to carousel to the Thrush Bank. When winter comes, however, most of the residents become "snow birds."

Birdhouse City is in the Macaulay Mountain Conservation Area on County Road 8.

"Empty nesters" in Picton's Birdhouse City.

The subdivision's wide streets give the historic community a modern appearance.

MARKHAM HERITAGE ESTATES:
A Suburb of Last Resort

Where do century-old farmhouses go when urban sprawl engulfs the cornfields? Sadly, most fall beneath the wrecker's ball to be replaced by an endless sea of look-alike new homes. But in the heritage-conscious community of Markham, historic houses are given a new lease on life.

Markham, a fast-growing area of big-box stores, endless malls and gridlocked traffic, sits on the northeastern fringe of the Greater Toronto Area. But despite this unchecked growth, Markham retains much of its built heritage.

That heritage dates back to the 1790s when William Berczy led a group of colonizers from the United States to the headwaters of the Rouge and Don rivers. In the years that followed, farm villages and mill towns appeared across the landscape. One of the most successful was Markham. In 1871 the Toronto and Nipissing Railway built a station a short distance north of Markham's mills, and the community boomed.

And thanks to Markham's citizens and politicians, much of that heritage has been retained. The historic main street, like that in the smaller village of Unionville a few kilometres west, has been historically refurbished, and new development must be compatible with the historic theme. North of the main street, the original station has been restored to its original appearance and reopened as a GO station and community facility.

And then there are the Markham Heritage Estates. Faced with the loss of countless historic farmhouses and village homes to urban sprawl, the Town of Markham gave the houses a home. In 1996, Markham created, adjacent to its museum village, a plan of a subdivision, with thirty-eight lots, solely for the purpose of relocating threatened heritage houses. Under the plan, the Town of Markham will sell the lots at less than market value to owners of heritage homes that are threatened with demolition. The amount saved on the price of the lot provides the owners with the incentive to relocate and restore the house in the new location.

Among the oldest of the relocated houses are the David Leek Houses built in 1840 and formerly located in the vanished village of Dollar, and the 1845 house built by Richard Lewis in the community of Gormley. For its heritage initiatives, Markham was awarded the coveted Prince of Wales Award.

Markham Heritage Estates is located next to 16th Avenue, west of Highway 48.

A GREEN SUDBURY

Could the barren moonscape once described as one of the world's worst environmental disasters ever be green again? So barren was the soil of Sudbury that American astronauts practised their moonwalks on the tormented terrain.

A century ago Sudbury was green. Pine forest covered the granite rocks. In 1883, the Canadian Pacific Railway blasted these rocks to make way for the national dream of a rail line to the Pacific, and the discovery of the world's largest deposit of copper and nickel in those rock cuts turned the little railway junction into a major mining town. But nickel refining is also one of the most polluting industries.

An obsolete process called "roasting" caused the damage. Crushed ore was laid on vast beds of burning cordwood. The roasting beds burned for months, sending billowing clouds of sulphur-laden smoke across the landscape. The smoke killed everything it touched. The refinery stacks were even worse, spewing tiny particles of nickel and copper oxide, which seeped into and poisoned the ground.

Trees were killed in all directions. The ground was barren. Nothing grew in the poisoned terrain.

Then, in 1969, when INCO constructed a superstack to spread the fumes further afield, local residents decided to make Sudbury green again. Although the first efforts at reforestation on the infertile ground were dismal failures, a few years later a Laurentian University biology professor began to experiment with lime. By laying down a layer of lime first, the poisons were neutralized. A variety of grasses were then planted. Once the grass took hold, the trees followed.

Schoolchildren, youth and miners all clambered over the hillsides and tailings, planting trees by the thousands. The efforts have won several national and international awards, including the Lieutenant Governor's Conservation Award, the United States Chevron Conservation Award, and the United Nations Local Government Honours Award, presented at the Earth Summit in Rio de Janeiro.

In 1997, the regional municipality unveiled a plaque beside its premier landmark, the Big Nickel, announcing the planting of the three millionth tree. Since that date, a further three million trees have been planted. Ironically, looming on the hill next to the plaque are the now-cleaned-up Inco stacks, and in between, a young forest of saplings that could only have been imagined a few years earlier.

Left: Once the area's major polluter, Inco's Sudbury stacks overlook a young forest.

Above: Three million trees have been replanted on what was once a barren, polluted moonscape.

CLIMBING NEPTUNE'S STAIRCASE:
The Welland Canals of St. Catharines

A good trivia question would be, "How many Welland Canals are there?" Most would say "one," and a few more knowledgeable souls might hazard "two." But the correct answer is "four."

Ground was broken for the first canal in 1824. A narrow ditch with wooden locks followed Twelve Mile Creek from Port Dalhousie to St. Catharines and up the Niagara Escarpment. From Port Robinson it followed Chippewa Creek—now the Welland River—to its first terminus at Chippewa, on the Niagara River. But it quickly became apparent that both the wooden locks and the route were inadequate.

In 1842 canal number two was begun. Open for business in 1851, it replaced the forty wooden locks with twenty-seven stone structures. Industries were built near the locks, and with the arrival of the railway, St. Catharines grew. But once more traffic outstripped capacity, and in 1872 yet a third canal was started.

The new route required only twenty-five locks. But it, too, was obsolete at the time it opened in 1881. Finally, in 1913, work started on number four, the Welland Ship Canal. Interrupted by the war, the canal finally opened in 1933. This time a completely new terminus was built at Port Weller, with a mere seven locks, twinned to allow more traffic. In 1973 a new bypass was constructed around Welland, giving the canal the current route.

But to history lovers the real attraction lies in the ruins of the early canals. Two parks provide particularly good opportunities to explore them. Princess Park, along Oakdale Avenue south of Westchester Avenue, displays a half dozen stone locks. Gateless but still sound, they function now as runoff channels. Near the corner of Bradley Street and Mountain Road is Mountain Locks Park. Nicknamed "Neptune's Staircase," a series of seven locks climbs the escarpment like a giant staircase. While the upper few locks flow with runoff, the lower portion is dry and lies overgrown in the woods.

At the few locales where it is visible, canal one is little more than a barely visible gully. However, the Welland Canal Society has reconstructed lock 28 of the first canal and excavated the wooden walls. It lies across the footbridge near the corner of Christina and Bradley. Nearby, two of the original lockmasters' houses are now private houses, at 77 and 135 Bradley Street.

The most remarkable aspect of the locks is their narrowness. Wide enough for a vessel the size of a modern motorboat, they emphasize how slow and arduous transportation must have been only a century and a half ago.

This abandoned lock from the second canal is one of the steps in a series of locks called Neptune's Staircase.

This mammoth open pit at Marmora is gradually filling with water.

MARMORA'S BIG HOLE

The huge pit may ultimately become Ontario's biggest pool. For as each year passes the gaping cavity left by the Marmoraton Iron Mine fills with a little more water. Though nobody will be swimming in it any day soon, it makes for one of Ontario's most unusual mining sights.

Mining days in Marmora date back to 1820. An iron magnate named Charles Hayes hacked a trail through the dark forests of central Hastings, hundreds of kilometres from the nearest city of any size. Here he began the construction of a mine, mill and smelter for the production of iron. The community of Marmora quickly grew to a population of two hundred.

For a time, Marmora and its neighbour Blairton, now a ghost town, were the leading iron producers in the country. Difficulty in transporting the iron out, however, proved their undoing. When canals were completed along the St. Lawrence River, cheaper iron could be imported, and Marmora's iron-mining days were over. Almost.

In 1949 an aeromagnetic survey revealed strange magnetic anomalies east of the town. Drilling quickly followed, revealing an immense body of ore, 700 metres long and 150 metres deep. The only problem was the 45 metres of limestone that lay on top of it.

In 1951, Bethlehem Steel Company began to haul away the intervening rock, and was soon removing a million tons of magnetic ore every year. Canadian National (CN) Railway trains carried it to the company's plant in Lackawanna, New York, where it was concentrated and pelletized. By the late 1970s the ore supply was exhausted, leaving a massive circular pit a third of a kilometre across and fully 200 metres deep.

During the mine's operation, a viewing area was provided so that the public could watch the monster trucks grind up out of the gaping hole, loaded with ore. Although the mine no longer operates, the viewing area reveals the emerging lake. The road to the viewing area leads south of Highway 7, just 1.4 kilometres east of the traffic lights in Marmora. Marmora's original iron smelter site is now marked by a plaque in a small park near the downtown area.

JAMES BOND AND THE SECRET OF CAMP X

Cloak-and-dagger movies and spy thrillers like the James Bond books conjure images of stealth, danger and sultry temptresses. In reality, undercover work was humdrum. Most espionage work involved censoring mail, breaking codes and forging diplomatic documents. Canada's most secret Second World War spy-training facility was known simply as Camp X.

Located on a then-isolated Lake Ontario shoreline, midway between Oshawa and Whitby, Camp X was the responsibility of a man called "Intrepid." In real life he was William (later Sir William) Stephenson. Born in Winnipeg, the decorated First World War flying ace was put in charge of British counterespionage at the camp.

The camp consisted of two components. One was the Special Training School, or STS 103, focussed on spy training. A second, even more secret activity, code-named Hydra, involved top-secret messages sent between the United States and Canada. So sensitive was the work that any outsiders who ventured near it were to be shot on sight.

After the war, Camp X continued as a government communications centre until 1969. Even then its wartime secrets remained locked away. Only after the buildings were demolished or removed were the secret activities at Camp X finally revealed.

While Stephenson became the subject of books (*A Man Called Intrepid*), another Camp X visitor went on to write them. Ian Fleming, a commander of British naval intelligence, used his spy training to create a fictional super spy named James Bond. While local speculation suggests that Fleming named his character after St. James Bond Church in Toronto, the more accepted version is that he borrowed the name of an ornithologist who authored the *Field Guide to the Birds of the West Indies*, a part of the world frequented by Fleming.

When the legends of Camp X finally became public, a park was opened on the site of the camp. Created in 1984, Intrepid Park features a large monument erected to commemorate those who worked there. On the base of the monument, photographs and text depict the story of the camp and its contribution to the Allied victory. From the monument, trails lead to an isolated beach on Lake Ontario, where artifacts from the camp, which had been dumped into the lake, wash ashore from time to time.

While most of the camp's buildings were demolished, some were removed to other sites. A former barracks is located at the Whitby Humane Society, on Thickson Road. A number of camp artifacts are on display at the Robert Stuart Aeronautical Museum at Oshawa Airport. No longer isolated, Camp X today is surrounded by industrial sprawl. The park and monument can be found on Boundary Road, on the Oshawa-Whitby border.

Other than the monument, little remains of Camp X, the top-secret war facility where James Bond was born in the mind of author Ian Fleming.

THE MAGICAL CYPRUS LAKE GROTTO

The timeless and irresistible forces of nature sometimes create magical landscapes. Few people enter a cave to go diving. Yet within the boundaries of one of Ontario's newest national parks, the Bruce Peninsula National Park, cave swimmers can dive into waters 12 metres deep. The grotto, at 20 metres long, ranges in width from 9 to 12 metres and looks out onto a small cove surrounded by rugged grey cliffs and a beach of broken boulders. Its isolation, its rugged beauty, and the tranquillity of a turquoise blue lagoon, make the setting almost magical.

For tens of thousands of years, the waves of Georgian Bay relentlessly pounded away at the limestone cliffs of the Bruce Peninsula. Deep inside, rainwater crept through cracks in the limestone to dissolve the rock from within. The result is a shoreline of cliffs, caves, the unusual rock pillars known as "flowerpots," and the Cyprus Lake Grotto. This outstanding assembly of unusual natural features, along with many rare species of flora and fauna, has long made the peninsula a popular destination for hikers and nature lovers.

Over the years, however, the lack of public land has hindered access for most. To remedy this, Parks Canada created a new national park to allow Canadians to experience one of their nation's great natural wonders. Local politics and hostility, however, prevented the park from taking in the entire northern peninsula. As a result, Bruce Peninsula National Park consists of three unconnected segments. The Fathom Five segment is set aside for divers to explore the underwater caves and shipwrecks, Flowerpot Island contains the best examples of these towering limestone pillars, while the Cypress Lake segment contains the grotto and shoreline.

Besides the grotto, trails lead to overhanging cliffs, underground passages and natural caves. The park is located on Highway 6 between Wiarton and Tobermory.

Limestone pillars known as "flowerpots" in Bruce Peninsula National Park.

85

SIZE MATTERS:
The Battle Over the Country's Smallest Jail

For many years, tourist brochures for the village of Tweed boasted of its having North America's smallest jail. The little stone lockup, then serving as a tourist information centre, measured a mere 4.9 metres by 6.1 metres. And for years the claim went unchallenged. Then several other communities began to discover that they, too, had little heritage jails, sometimes literally in their own backyards.

Creemore jumped in with its jail of 4.5 metres by 6.0 metres. Located beside the library, a block east of the main street, it now serves as a museum. The tiny cells remain as they were when they held the local town drunk (or, in one case, a cow).

Down a small side street in Coboconk, a little stone building was scheduled for demolition. A local seniors' group lobbied for its preservation, and so the "Coby" jail was saved. Its dimensions, however, proved to be a few centimetres shorter than that in Creemore, and today it functions as a gift shop run by the same seniors' group.

Deep in southwestern Ontario, the little railway town of Rodney also has its own tiny claim to fame—a brick jail beside the fairgrounds that measures a mere 4.5 metres by 5.4 metres. After serving as a book drop for many years, it is now a tourist information centre, although only seldom open.

Port Dalhousie, near St. Catharines, was not to be outdone and submitted its own candidate with measurements almost identical to those of the Rodney jail. It is now part of a bar. Also, almost forgotten, and unacclaimed, is the former jail in Providence Bay on Manitoulin Island, which is now converted to a cabin for tourists.

But the smallest of them all, and virtually inaccessible, is the one-cell lockup in the ghost town of Barens River. A short-lived gold-mining town, it lies on an isolated lake far to the north of Red Lake, and is accessible only by float plane.

And as for the original claimant in Tweed—it's now back in business as a community police station!

The tiny Creemore lockup is one of several claiming to be North America's smallest.

86

Woodchester Villa, Bracebridge

EIGHT SIDES TO A HOUSE:
Woodchester Villa

During the first two generations of Ontario's European settlement, house styles were fairly uniform; from log cabins to Georgian mansions, the pattern was consistently boxy. But with affluence and stability, and with the increasing artistic curiosity of the Victorian age, there came more architectural experimentation. This brought one of the more unusual house styles ever seen in Ontario, and indeed in northeastern North America, the eight-sided house.

The origin of the design is credited to an amateur architect, American Orson Fowler, who featured it in his 1848 book, *A Home for All*. Its advantages, he argued, were that a greater floor-space-to-wall-space ratio made it cheaper to build, and with more external wall space for windows, it was brighter and therefore healthier.

Henry Bird apparently agreed. In 1882, he built one of Ontario's first octagonal houses, in what was then a raw frontier town named Bracebridge. The owner of a large woollen mill, Bird built his home near the pioneer Muskoka Road, on a hill overlooking the town. The eight walls alternated between 5 metres and 4.5 metres wide, and were nearly a half metre thick. The house remained in the Bird family for nearly a century, until it was sold to a local service club and shortly thereafter opened as a museum.

The style had many imitators, and by 1900 Ontario could boast more than one hundred octagonal houses. Today fewer than half remain, most in central or eastern Ontario, including Lowville, Huttonville, Maple, Picton, Calabogie and Hawkesbury, the latter town also claiming an octagonal barn. Ontario's northernmost multi-sided building is the popular round barn near Sault Ste. Marie, on the Trans-Canada Highway.

Woodchester Villa is located on King Street, close to the historic alignment of the Muskoka Road, although the steepness of the hill here closed the through route.

With its five stone arches, the Pakenham Bridge is the only of its kind in North America.

PAKENHAM'S STONE ARCH BRIDGE:
North America's Longest

Among Ontario's heritage features, bridges are the least appreciated; yet Ontario boasts many distinctive bridges. For example, North America's longest wooden bridge crosses Sioux Narrows in northwestern Ontario; West Montrose, near Kitchener, is the only remaining covered bridge in Ontario; and a railway swing bridge provides the only road access to Manitoulin, the world's largest freshwater island. One of the most beautiful of Ontario's bridges is Pakenham's bridge, the only five-span stone arched bridge in North America.

Built in 1901, it replaced a rickety wooden structure. The old bridge was so unsafe that it was illegal to cross "at a faster pace than a walk." Designed by the firm of O'Toole and Keating, the new 85-metre bridge is made up of five 25-metre stone arches on piers that are 3 metres thick. The huge stones for the bridge were dragged from a nearby quarry. The largest stone is 3 metres long by nearly a metre square, and weighs 5 tonnes.

In 1984, Ontario's Ministry of Transportation, along with the Ontario Heritage Foundation and Ottawa's National Capital Commission, restored the bridge, inserting reinforced concrete into the deck and parapet walls in the stonework. Framed by its wooded limestone shoreline, the bridge is a popular subject for photographers and artists.

Pakenham village itself is also worth a visit. Despite its location, well inland from Ontario's first towns and villages, Pakenham got off to an early start. By 1831 it had become the site of a sawmill, store and post office, and was named Little Falls. In 1840, Andrew Dickson sold the first village lots, and just twenty years later the village claimed a population of eight hundred. Despite getting the railway in the 1880s, Pakenham failed to grow, and the population is about the same today, which has helped preserve its rich heritage.

On the main street, only a short distance from the bridge, are businesses such as Byrne House Hardware, housed in a mid-1800s Classical Revival building; Paddye Mann Designs in an 1830s stone building; and Ontario's "oldest" general store. Built in 1840, Pakenham's general store contains crafts, memorabilia, and freshly baked breads, as well as the usual range of grocery items. On the opposite side of the bridge, the Stone Bridge Shop operates from a converted 1842 gristmill.

Pakenham is on Highway 15 about halfway between Almonte and Arnprior, and about 60 kilometres west of downtown Ottawa. Caution should be used if crossing the bridge on foot; there is no sidewalk, the roadway is narrow, and County Road 20 can be busy.

ONTARIO'S WORST ROADS:
The Forgotten Corduroy Trails

No matter how much we deride our deteriorating roads, with their washboards and potholes, no road was more painful to travel than the corduroy roads of pioneer Ontario. To allow horses and wagons to cross low-lying areas, which were bogs during the spring season, logs were laid side by side. The effect resembled the ridged cloth preferred by European royalty, and they were named "corduroy" or "cords-du-roi" roads.

The first roads in Ontario simply followed the trails tramped by the Aboriginal inhabitants. These followed the higher grounds between main waterways and avoided obstacles. Then, as the surveyors marched through the forests, clearing the first military roads, they cared little for anything that got in the way, and laid the roads with straight military precision. Swamps were simply dealt with by the use of the hated log roads.

Early pioneer diaries lamented the tossing and the lurching that tormented their authors as they bounced over the irregular and rotting sections of corduroy. Eventually, as more settlers arrived, the roads were graded and gravelled, and finally, with the advent of the auto age, paved.

Not too surprisingly, the original log trails are nearly impossible to find anymore. Not only has rot and resurfacing obliterated them, but they have been almost totally ignored by heritage preservationists, which makes the few places where they can still be seen unusual.

One of the clearest and longest stretches of such road lies on a hiking trail in Awenda Provincial Park, north of Midland. It was once used as a logging road through this forested recreation area. In Killarney Provincial Park, the Silhouette Trail includes corduroy logging roads as well, as does the trail in Rawhide Conservation Area, 35 kilometres north of Elliot Lake. Parts of Muskoka Road 14 between Fraserburg and Pine Lake have been neglected to the point that the old logs are making their way to the surface, to the dismay of local residents. Also in Muskoka, the Buckwallow Trail follows corduroy sections of the original Peterson Colonization Road. And in the Beaver Valley, east of Kimberley, another old section of corduroy road forms part of a local trail. Likely there remain other long-forgotten segments of log road that lurk yet on abandoned portions of Ontario's earliest roads.

Logs peek through the soil on this rare example of a surviving corduroy road.

The flag station at Union, still in use, is North America's smallest "Union Station."

THE SMALLEST UNION STATION

What is the size of a two-hole outhouse and attracts tourists from across the continent? The answer is North America's smallest "Union Station." In railway terminology, a union station is one shared by more than one railway company, and more often than not they are large, urban terminals. Therefore, when train travellers think of Union Station, they picture the high-vaulted concourse of Toronto's Union Station, or the grand facade of that in Washington, D.C. They are not likely to envisage the tiny grey-flag station that guards the track of the Port Stanley Terminal Railway. The station's name derives not from its size or its function, but simply from the name of a nearby hamlet, Union.

Not only is it the oldest building on the once-busy line, but the style and the arched windows reveal that railway architects often paid as much attention to the tiny flag stations as they did to the larger and more elegant city stations.

Today's Port Stanley Terminal Railway was resurrected as a labour of love from the near ruins of the pioneering London and Port Stanley Railway. Originally built to carry lumber and farm products from the southwestern farmlands to the wharves at Port Stanley, and to link with the Grand Trunk Railway in London, it eventually became a busy excursion line. Londoners crowded into the coaches at that city's now long-demolished brick-and-stone station to go to the Lake Erie beaches, or to dance to the big bands that played the internationally renowned Stork Club.

Eventually CN took over the line and, after a few years of dwindling traffic, closed it. While other stations were demolished, the little flag station at Union was given little thought. When the line was abandoned, Union Station, deteriorating and overgrown, miraculously still stood.

Local rail enthusiasts purchased the line and, after pouring countless hours and money from their own pockets into its repair, have restored passenger rides from Port Stanley to the south end of St. Thomas. Awaiting the passengers halfway along is the smallest Union Station, restored, repainted, and housing old photos and railway memorabilia.

You can board the excursion trains at the larger station in Port Stanley and travel the few miles up the line to Union and St. Thomas, or, if the trains aren't running that day, you can follow the Golf Club Road west to the little station from Highway 4 in Union.

THE FEELING OF BEING WATCHED:
Toronto's Old City Hall Gargoyles

Have you ever had the feeling that you're being watched? Stand in front of Toronto's Old City Hall and you are—by its gargoyles!

Old City Hall is a remarkable example of the Victorian Romanesque Revival architectural style. Completed in 1899, it was one of those grand municipal buildings typical of the period. With its tall clock tower dominating Bay Street, each nook and cranny—and there are many—of its sandstone exterior seems to offer a different architectural surprise, especially the gargoyles. While such grotesque faces were common on medieval buildings, some of those on Old City Hall carried a special meaning.

City architect E. J. Lennox had staked much of his reputation on what he hoped would be his masterpiece. But when the Toronto city council of the day short-changed him, or so he thought, he decided to even the score. There, above the grand entrance, sits E. J. Lennox's revenge: the gargoyles are the distorted faces of the councillors themselves. In a final act of defiance, Lennox added, contrary to instructions, his own name and a caricature said to resemble himself. Old City Hall is festooned with dozens of the more traditional gargoyles—grotesque animal-like faces. But the faces of the Toronto council of the day will live on in a way none had likely intended.

Much of Victorian Toronto has vanished. Fine old buildings of stone or brick have fallen victim to insensitive redevelopment, and to builders whose bottom line doesn't include a respect for heritage. Even Old City Hall itself was threatened when the Eaton Centre was proposed. But citizen outrage saved the building, which today functions as a court. And so, amid modern glass and concrete towers, the gargoyles of Toronto's Old City Hall still keep watch.

The faces of Old City Hall.

KAPUSKASING:
A Planned Town in the Northern Bush

West of Cochrane, in northeastern Ontario, Highway 11 lies straight and flat, flanked on one side by abandoned farmland and on the other by a single, lonely railway track. A short distance north, a low woodland stretches unbroken to Hudson Bay. It is, in other words, the least likely place to find Ontario's first modern planned town.

Kapuskasing began innocuously as MacPherson Siding in 1913 on the newly completed National Transcontinental Railway. Its isolation made it ideal for a prisoner-of-war camp during the First World War. Following the war, returning soldiers were directed to what was touted as "New Ontario," where the flat, stone-free soils of the Great Clay Belt would spawn a prosperous new agricultural community. But even an agricultural experimental farm could not overcome the harsh climate and the unrelenting flies, and most of the fledgling farmers returned south.

Had it not been for the Kapuskasing Pulp and Timber Company, that might have been the end of the settlement; however, the water power of the falls in the Kapuskasing River and the level terrain on the riverbank convinced the company to locate its mill and workers here. Anxious to justify its interest in the new north, the Ontario government undertook to build the company a new town, and it was to be the best. It would be a planned town—a model for future modern towns, and would contain gardens, Tudor architecture and streets that would radiate from a central circle.

By 1923, Kapuskasing, with its new brick railway station, was complete. The Kapuskasing Inn, with its grand Tudor gables, and the recreation centre (later the town hall) gazed over the landscaped banks of a bay in the river, while the equally grand hospital dominated a triangular green common. Businesses grouped around the circle in the centre of town, while stately homes flanked the curving streets.

In eighty years, "Kap" has changed modestly. Although highway businesses now stretch out along Highway 11, the circle remains the heart of the community, dominated now by a fountain. Former shanty towns that clung to its fringes have been incorporated and upgraded. Although passenger train service was discontinued in 1980, the station survives as a private business and bus terminal, beside it the preserved engine and coaches that make up the Ron Morel Museum.

For all the changes, Kapuskasing, surrounded by the remains of a failed farming scheme, faded railway towns, and seemingly endless bushland, remains the anomaly of the North.

The Kapuskasing Inn displays its Tudoresque style in this unusual northern town.

Shanty's Bay Anglican church is North America's only example of a "mud church."

THE MUD CHURCH OF SHANTY BAY

Canadians have long looked to nature for building material. Bark and skins were used by Aboriginal inhabitants. The first shanties of the European arrivals were hastily erected from logs, while prairie pioneers were noted for their early sod huts. And where stones were plentiful they were used for homes, mills, churches and schools.

While adobe brick was commonly used in the southwestern U.S., it was rarely employed in Canada, due largely to its vulnerability to rain. But one ingredient was so rarely used that only one building of any significance in Canada is known to have used it, and that ingredient is mud.

Common in medieval Europe, it is also known as cob, or "rammed earth" construction, and consists of a mixture of clay, sand and straw. The three ingredients are mixed into a dough-like substance and pressed, or rammed, into a wall mould. It is then covered with plaster or wood to protect the mud from deterioration. The only building of such size to be made of the mud, some say in all of North America, is St. Thomas Anglican Church in a hamlet on the north shore of Lake Simcoe named Shanty Bay.

The church was started in 1837 on land donated by the founder of the Shanty Bay settlement, Colonel Edward O'Brien. The mud walls, 1 metre thick, were laid on a stone foundation. Wood was hand hewn from local supplies of pine, ash and cedar—the axe marks remain visible to this day. The original square pews are still used as well.

Despite the unusual construction technique, you wouldn't know it to look at it. With its stucco finish, it resembles many a church of the era, solid and Gothic, with a handsome steeple. In only a few sections of the lower wall is the mud exposed.

The church, which remains in full use, lies south of Ridge Road in the centre of the village, about 8 kilometres east of Barrie. The name of the village itself dates to the 1830s as well, when the community was a jumping-off point for black settlers en route to farm lots north of the lake. Their settlement has also left its religious imprint in the Oro African Church, built in 1848 and located on the Old Barrie Road at the east end of the village of Edgar, about 10 kilometres from Shanty Bay.

THE GUILD INN'S GARDEN OF RUINS

High atop the rugged cliffs of Toronto's Scarborough Bluffs is a garden with some very unusual decorations—the ruins of demolished buildings. The clifftop property was bought by Colonel Harold Bickford, who built a thirty-three-room Georgian villa as a country home, calling it Raneleigh Park. Following a series of owners, the place was finally bought by Rose Breithaupt Hewetson in 1932. After her marriage to Herbert Spencer Clark, the couple established the Guild of All Arts. They added cabins and workshops for artists who, in the Depression years, would have had no studio space.

They then added more living quarters, and with the increasing numbers of visitors, gradually converted it into a country inn with a restaurant. However, the war saw the guild taken over as a hospital, and it was not returned to the Clarks until 1947.

In the early 1950s, taxes forced the Clarks to sell all but 90 acres around the villa where, exasperated by the rampant demolition of Toronto's heritage buildings, they began to acquire vestiges of the vanishing structures. Soon the ruins became an attraction in their own right. A modern hotel was added in the 1960s, attracting conventions and workshops. Finally, in 1978, the entire property was purchased by the Metro Region Conservation Authority, and the grounds were opened to the public.

In the late 1990s, the hotel and restaurant were closed while new operators were sought. Despite the closure, the Garden of Ruins remained a public park. Among the ruins are a lion's-head keystone from the downtown plant of the O'Keefe Brewery, and an archway and columns from the Bank of Toronto, which have become the most photographed subject on the property and are particularly popular for wedding photographers and movie shoots. Two dozen vestiges are spread around the landscaped flower and shrub gardens, coming from canals, mills, post offices and even old high schools.

The Guild Inn is located on the Guildwood Parkway, south of Kingston Road.

The rescued remains of Toronto's demolished buildings decorate the Guild Inn's gardens.

A LEGACY IN LOG:
The Madill Church

When pioneers cleared the forests and broke the soil, their first buildings were hastily built of the closest material at hand—logs. Shanties had to make do until a larger, second home could be built, also of logs. Once the farmers became established they added their third house, now more substantial and built with more durable materials such as stone, brick or planks.

Throughout most of Ontario the log era has long passed. However, in the Ottawa Valley and the rugged uplands of Muskoka there remains a log legacy that includes barns, houses, churches, schools, general stores and hotels. Near Petawawa, west of Ottawa, stands a log hotel with its stables, all dating from the days of stage travel. Known as the Ferguson Stopping Place, it is now a bed and breakfast. On the grounds of the Waba Cottage Museum are a relocated log school and church.

A tour of almost any country road in the Ottawa Valley will reveal a form of barn known as the "string" barn. Where farmers could ill afford to replace their first log barns, they simply added to them, creating a string of barns that usually enclosed their animal pens.

The village of Burnstown, perched on a wall of the Madawaska River Canyon, boasts a log general store, while the village of Ashton can claim nearly half of its homes as log. Even Ottawa itself hides a pair of original log houses, both within a few paces of the popular downtown Byward Market.

Muskoka, too, celebrates its own log legacy with churches near Southwood, Bracebridge, Sand Lake and Rosseau; however, the best-known and most-visited is the Gothic log church founded by John Madill in 1873. It lies on the west side of the historic Muskoka Colonization Road at the Madill Church Road, a short distance west of Highway 11.

The Madill Church is a reminder of central Ontario's log legacy.

Castle Kilbride is a Baden landmark.

3-D-CEPTION:
The Trompe l'Oeil Murals of Castle Kilbride

Like most nineteenth-century mansions, Castle Kilbride is a monument to the excesses of the Industrial Age. Born to a Scottish weaver, James Livingston arrived in Canada in 1854 at the age of sixteen, where he worked first on a farm, then in a flax mill. In 1864, along with his brother, he rented a flax mill in the village of Wellesley. Within just three years the pair had built their own flax mill in Baden, adding a linseed-oil mill to their operation. Linseed oil was a key ingredient in paint and soap, and in high demand in Ontario's booming cities.

In 1877, Livingston, known as the "Flax and Oil King of Canada," decided to build his "castle." Set back from the road, surrounded by a wrought-iron fence and topped with an Italianate belvedere, Castle Kilbride quickly became a local landmark.

The elegance was evident on the exterior, but it was the inside that drew the most attention. Created by a local artist who signed his name as "Schasstein," three-dimensional murals, known by the French term trompe l'oeil, were painted on the mansion's walls and many of its ceilings. In the main hall, Schasstein created columns, statues and vases, all seemingly three-dimensional. More await in the library, where 3-D tassels surround the ceiling, framing cornices, mouldings and more murals.

In 1988, the castle and its grounds were sold to a developer and its contents auctioned. But as so often happens in small communities, the local residents were not about to let their most prominent building disappear. In 1993, the Township of Wilmot bought the property and began restoration. By holding a celebrity auction, they were able to recover many of the original contents, including an old toy collection. New municipal offices were added to the back of the building, and the interior was brought up to museum standards. A gift shop and washrooms were also added (although the original two-hole brick outhouse still stands outside).

Due largely to the remarkable murals, Parks Canada has declared the building a National Historic Site. The castle is located on Regional Road 1.

TEMAGAMI'S TALL PINES

The stately white pine, Ontario's provincial tree, is threatened with extinction, thanks to the cutting plans devised by Ontario's Ministry of Natural Resources, along with the logging interests. The few remaining stands represent a mere 1 percent of the pine forest's original extent, and that makes them a rare heritage legacy. Many of those tall pines are to be found in the Temagami area of northeastern Ontario.

Situated about two hour's drive north of North Bay, the area contains a wilderness relic, with lakes and rivers surrounded by tall-pine forests. Of Temagami's tall pine areas, the Lady Evelyn Smoothwater Park, accessible only by water, is perhaps the best known (although even it is now part of a ministry cutting plan).

A lesser-known tall-pine area, however, is easily accessible right within the limits of the village, and can be reached on foot. Known as the White Bear Forest, it takes its name from the last chief of a local tribe that used the area for hunting and trapping. In 1928, logging began on 500 square kilometres. But the company, run by the Gillies Brothers, decided to set aside the 800-hectare White Bear Forest as a reminder of what the ancient forests once looked like.

And it is here that the pines still loom large. The forest is the sixth largest old-growth white-pine forest still known, and, more remarkably, is the most accessible. Several kilometres of trail wind through the forest and can be accessed by car from the Caribou Mountain Ski Hill, or by boat from Northland Paradise Lodge on Snake Island Lake, which can also be reached by car. The trails range from one to two-and-a-half hours hiking duration. While many ecological features dot the routes, from red-pine stands to beaver meadows, the highlight is the grove of soaring white pines on the north shore of Pleasant Lake (although they are found throughout the reserve). The forest also offers scenic lookouts and a preserved fire tower.

The village of Temagami, on Highway 11, contains a pair of small restaurants, a motel, access to several lodges, and a revitalized waterfront. The village's heritage centrepiece, however, is the historic Temiskaming & Northern Ontario (T & NO) railway station, now being restored by a local restoration trust. The Tudor-style stone station is one the most attractive in northern Ontario, and still offers a waiting room for passengers on the daily Northlander train.

The White Bear tall pine forest at Temagami.

TINY TOWN:
Toronto's Smallest Houses

Toronto's little nooks and crannies hide many surprises. While its older and architecturally more splendid buildings are widely known, smaller and simpler structures are often even more interesting because their odds of surviving demolition or alteration are comparatively slim. That's the case with Cabbagetown's tiny Wellesley Cottages, located just north of Wellesley Street at Sackville.

During the 1870s and '80s, Ontario's railway boom years, labourers' cottages, as they were called, were hastily built to house the influx of workers. Between then and the 1890s, thousands were constructed in working-class neighbourhoods all across Toronto. The Wellesley Cottages were built around 1886–87.

Constructed of wood, usually with no foundations, these tiny one-and-a-half-storey cabins all boasted a centre plan, and many had a trademark gable over the front door. The style earned its designers an architectural award for workmen's cottage design at the Crystal Palace Exhibit in England in 1851.

Over the years, demands for bigger and safer housing meant the end of a housing era in Toronto and the gradual disappearance of these simple abodes. Throughout the city now only a few isolated examples survive, and the Wellesley Cottages are a remarkable row of seven. They are located, not on a main residential street, but on a narrow lane behind the backyards of the principal row of houses. After being used for a time as low-cost rental units, they were sold to a developer who upgraded them, a trend in Cabbagetown, which since the 1970s has become extensively gentrified.

Much of Old Cabbagetown is equally interesting. A stroll along Wellesley, Sumach (Cabbagetown's old-timers pronounce it "shoo-mack"), Spruce and Winchester streets reveals a residential neighbourhood of eclectic houses that date to the days when the area's low-income residents planted cabbages in their front yards, giving the community its unusual name. In this area you will also find the former Riverdale Zoo, now an animal farm for children, and the Spruce Court apartments, built in 1913 as Toronto's first government-sponsored housing project.

A few blocks to the south, in an area of Cabbagetown replaced in the late 1940s by low-cost apartments, is Toronto's "smallest" house. Built in about 1885, 383 Shuter Street measures a mere 2.5 metres wide. It remained a single-storey dwelling until 1981, when extra floors were added. If basketball great Wilt Chamberlain were to lie crossways in it, he would have no room to stretch!

Another row of tiny nineteenth-century homes lines a narrow lane a block west of McCaul and a short distance north of Queen.

Toronto's tiny Wellesley cottages.

DEPOT HARBOUR:
A Ghost Town Worth Visiting

For ghost-town enthusiasts, the Parry Sound area offers Ontario's richest ghost-town grounds, and one of its most rewarding ghost-town sites. During its heyday, Depot Harbour was a busy railway terminus and Great Lakes port, and with sixteen hundred residents it threatened to eclipse places like Midland and Owen Sound. But today the wind blows across cracked sidewalks and overgrown foundations, as Georgian Bay's waves now lap against silent shores.

It all began in the 1890s when lumber baron John Rudolphus Booth forged a rail link across the middle of Ontario from Ottawa to Georgian Bay and through Algonquin Park. His Ottawa, Arnprior and Parry Sound Railway would thereby not only access his rich pine limits in the park, but would also give Canada's western grain growers their most direct route to the ice-free Atlantic Ocean ports.

A dispute over the location of the terminus on Georgian Bay led Booth to seek a site where he could build his own town. On Parry Island, beside the Great Lake's largest natural harbour, Booth built the town of Depot Harbour. The town contained three churches, a school, railway yards and a roundhouse, two large grain elevators and more than one hundred dwellings.

For three decades the place prospered and seemed destined to become one of the busiest ports on the Great Lakes. Then, in 1928, the Canadian National Railway, which had by then assembled a collection of bankrupt rail lines, amalgamated its facilities at a location south of Parry Sound. Five years later an ice floe damaged a trestle in Algonquin Park and CN simply closed the route.

The lifeline of Depot Harbours was severed, a calamity from which it never recovered. In 1945, the port facilities, which were then storing the volatile cordite for a nearby munitions factory, erupted in a midnight fireball that lit up the streets of Parry Sound, 10 kilometres away. Depot Harbour's story was over. The houses were sold off for $25 each and moved away.

By the 1960s only the Catholic church, the shell of the roundhouse, and a single dwelling remained standing. Today, the roundhouse alone survives. Beyond it, hidden by a forest now a half century old, lie the foundations, the old sidewalks, the remains of the company vault, and the massive wharf, all now silent. Although the ruins become more and more obscured as the years pass, it remains Ontario's most extensive ghost town. In 1996, the townsite reverted to the ownership of the island's First Nations band.

The grey arches of a one-time railway roundhouse peer from the woods at the site of the once bustling port of Depot Harbour.

THE RETURN OF MUSKOKA'S PORTAGE FLYER:

The World's Shortest Railway

It has come back home. Following an absence of more than forty years, the famed *Portage Flyer* has returned to Muskoka. Once deemed the world's shortest commercial railway, the Huntsville and Lake of Bays Railway was a fixture on the landscape from 1904, when it began shuttling steamboat passengers between Peninsula Lake and Lake of Bays.

Although the Muskoka Lakes region had become a haven for tourists, roads and cars were many years in the future. Travellers would arrive by train and then transfer onto steamers for the trip to the many grand hotels that ringed the lakes. While vacationers could transfer easily from the Grand Trunk trains in Huntsville onto steamers bound for Fairy and Peninsula lakes, there remained a difficult height of land barring the route to the lovely Lake of Bays. A plan to connect Bracebridge to the lake by rail was scrapped when the steamboat company decided to link the lakes with a much shorter portage railway.

The narrow line had to climb more than 40 metres, doing so in just 3 kilometres. A pair of steam locomotives hauled two passenger coaches, which were converted from old Toronto streetcars. These were replaced in 1948 by newer engines. But the end of the era was in sight, and a decade later the Muskoka District had been infiltrated by new paved roads. Rather than taking steamers to lodges, city dwellers were packing their cars and driving to private cottages instead.

Steamers were floated into dry docks and scrapped; lodges were burned or demolished, and in 1959, the *Portage Flyer* made its last run. The equipment was sold and removed. For several years it was a popular attraction at Pinafore Park in St. Thomas. Finally, in 1984, the volunteer-run Huntsville and Lake of Bays Railway Society bought the old rolling stock and brought it back to Huntsville.

Finally, on June 1, 2000, the *Portage Flyer* once more puffed into service. The new route begins at the Muskoka Heritage Park in Huntsville, where a new two-storey station houses a waiting room, ticket office and historic photos, as well as community meeting rooms on the second floor. The trains now follow a 1.25-kilometre route along the banks of the Muskoka River to the shore of Fairy Lake, where the purser's cabin from the dock of a nearby hotel on Fairy Lake has become the Fairy Lake "station." To house the heritage rolling stock, the volunteers erected an engine shed and 500 metres of siding. The station is located on Brunel Street in Huntsville.

The historic *Portage Flyer* is ready to ride again.

100

Along one of Ontario's most unusual roads, the river level is higher than the fields.

THE LEVEE ROAD

While the length of the road is short, it displays a landscape that few in Ontario could imagine exists, one that is reminiscent of a scene in Holland. This is a road that follows the top of a dyke, or levee. On the south side of the road, the waters of the Thames River lap at the level of the shoulder. On the north side, however, the shoulder drops down 5 metres to a plain of crops that stretches flat to a nearly treeless horizon.

Here, where the Thames River flows into Lake St. Clair, was a rare region of prairie, the most extensive in Ontario. So alluring was the lack of a forest cover that in 1804 Alexander Selkirk brought several families from the highlands of Scotland to settle in a agricultural colony called the Baldoon Settlement.

It seemed too good to be true, and it was. When the settlers moved onto their farm, the waters of Lake St. Clair were abnormally low. As they rose to more normal levels, the water inundated the fields, bringing disease to livestock and settlers alike. Then, during the War of 1812, invading American armies pillaged the farms, and soon the colony was abandoned.

Still, the extensive prairie lands were stone free and fertile, and the area's growing season was the longest in Ontario. Drainage schemes kept the lake waters at bay, and soon the region had become Ontario's main producer of sugar beets, a crop that provided the economic mainstay for a series of French Canadian villages like Paincourt and Grand Pointe.

But the Thames River had yet to be tamed. Severe flooding in 1937, and again a decade later, put thousands of hectares of land under water. Then, with a rise in the level of Lake St. Clair between 1964 and 1973, the federal and provincial governments embarked upon a scheme to construct a line of levees along the lower Thames River, as well as on portions of its branches, Jeanette Creek and Baptiste Creek. In all, more than 56 kilometres of dyking was constructed to protect more than 9,000 hectares of farmland.

While sections of Grand River Road and County Road 36 parallel the levees west of the city of Chatham, an extension of Grand River Road, between Jacob Road and Town Line Road, follows the top of the levee itself.

Although the natural prairie ecology has long vanished, the scene is indeed prairie-like, with flat, dark soils stretching to a treeless horizon, where the main visual intrusions are the sugar-beet silos. It is a scene unlike any other in Ontario.

INDEX

Answer to the Bean Cryptogram

Starting with the letter "I," read in a zig-zag counter-clockwise direction and the following dedication appears:

"In memoriam Henrietta, 1st wife of S. Bean. M.D. who died 27th Sep 1865 aged 23 years 2 months and 17 days & Susanna his second wife who died 27th April 1867 aged 26 years 3 months and 15 days.

2 better wives 1 man never had. They were gifts from God and are now in Heaven. May God help me S.B. to meet them there."